The EU: A Corporatist Racket

The real but startling story of Britain's entry into the Common Market in the early 1970s

by

David Barnby

Orinoco Standard

Cover by John Leftwich

*The electorate expect that those
we elect will make our laws –
is that too much to ask?*

The Author

David Barnby recalls being taught at school that Britain had over the centuries, developed the concepts of freedom and democracy which the rest of the world had adopted. A keen observer of Prime Minister Harold Macmillan's attempt to join the European Economic Community (EEC) in the early 1960s, he was disappointed when General de Gaulle, the President French, vetoed Britain's application in February 1963. However, it was with concern that, after eventual entry in 1973, new treaties were entered into without consultation of the electorate and without reference to the Constitution. It was when Prime Minister John Major whipped the Treaty of Maastricht through Parliament in 1992, which, again, was contrary to the Constitution and which handed unprecedented powers to an unelected and unaccountable bureaucracy in Brussels that he turned against membership of what had by then become the EU. When Foreign Office records became available under the 30 year rule in 2003, he carried out a detailed study of Edward Heath's campaign that led to Britain's membership. This study resulted in the popular CD: '*Shoe-horned into the EU*'. Since that time he has come to understand that it is global corporate interests that were and are behind the demise of freedom and democracy that joining bodies like the EU entail. This book is adapted from '*Shoe-horned*', with extensive research material added in chapters to be found in Part II of this book so as to justify the new title: '*A Corporatist Racket*'.

Main UK distributor
The June Press
PO Box 119
Totnes
Devon TQ9 7WA
Tel: 44(0)8456 120 175
Fax : 44(0)8456 120 176
Email : info@junepress.com
Web : www.junepress.com

Cover by John Leftwich

ISBN 978-0-9569815-8-5

The EU: A Corporatist Racket

Orinoco Standard
Published by David Barnby, Witney
davebarnby@aol.com
Copyright © 2015

CONTENTS

Acknowledgements and Sources   i

Preface   iv

Introduction   xi

PART I

PM, Edward Heath's Campaign to take Britain into the EEC 1970-1972

Diagram – Follow the Money

Chapter.1   No loss of essential Sovereignty   1

Chapter.2 Heath's Campaign 1970 - 1972   4
    The Players
    The Public Campaign

Chapter.3 The Civil Service in Action   8

    The Foreign and Commonwealth Office (FCO)
    Broadcast Media Participation
    FCO Conspires to Neutralise the Keep Britain
    Out Campaign
    Tracking Enoch Powell

Chapter.4 Jean Monnet and his Comité d'Action pour les   25
          États-Unis d'Europe

Chapter.5 The mysterious cancellation of Black Arrow –   30
          Britain's last Satellite launcher rocket

Chapter.6 The British Council of the European Movement   46
          (BCEM)

Chapter.7 Participation by Brussels   56

Chapter.8 Town Twinning   58

Chapter.9 Convincing Conservative rank and file   61

Chapter.10 Resisting a referendum on joining   63

Chapter.11 The Parliamentary 'Stitch-up'   67
    Conservative Whip's Report – free or whipped vote?

Whips' Report – pressure on Conservative elected representatives
European Communities Bill (1972) Second Reading - Hansard
The motion was passed by 301 votes to 309 votes

Chapter.12 The Questions then...   81

PART II

European Integration, the broader picture – 1948 -2014

Chapter.1   ACUE and the European Movement   83

Chapter.2   Consolidation – the meaning of June 5th, 1975   95
            Referendum

Chapter.3   FCO 30-1048, the Heath Government knew it   109
            would lead to a loss of sovereignty

Chapter.4   Pressure in constituencies – Neil Marten   116

Chapter.5   85 Frampton Street   121

Chapter.6   European Communities Act 1972 – Lord Pearson 128

Chapter.7   World Economic Forum – Strategic partners   130

Chapter.8   Bilderberg   135

Chapter.9   Profile of a Pro-European   156

Postscript: The Rats   160

Bibliography   168

Index   172

Introduction

Britain emerged from a six year struggle with Germany and its allies, Italy and Japan in August 1945, exhausted and virtually bankrupt. Britain had, together with its empire, been in the fight from start to finish maintaining the flame of freedom and democracy for Europe and the hope for a better world to come.

The Soviet Union as it was then known had without doubt borne the greatest burden in the Second World War and the United States, entering the war late, provided massive military power that enabled the Allies to overwhelm the armies, navies and air-forces ranged against it.

Victory came at a cost to Britain by incurring huge indebtedness, particularly to the Americans who had supplied vast quantities of military hardware and other resources for its war effort. On the other hand the United States came out of the conflict immensely wealthier[1]. It had previously suffered the economic stagnation of the great depression that had continued almost up to the start of the Second World War.

In Britain, it was expected and earnestly hoped that the end of the war would see social justice firmly on the agenda together with an improvement in general living standards. Conditions did slowly improve and the advent of the National Health Service (NHS), social and technological advances, eventually led to a nation better off than it had been before the war[2].

The promise though was in many ways not fulfilled as the so called

---

[1] Sterling and Peggy Seagrave in their book 'Gold Warriors' claim the USA acquired large amounts of gold and other treasures at the defeat of Japan and Germany in 1945: 'The treasure. .... was combined with Axis loot recovered in Europe to create a worldwide covert political fund to fight communism. This 'black gold' gave the Truman Administration access to virtually limitless unvouchered funds for covert operations. It also provided an asset base .... to bribe political leaders, and to manipulate elections in foreign countries.' Also see: Nazi Gold: The Merkers Mine Treasure by Greg Bradsher; Prologue Magazine, Spring 1999, Vol.31, No.1 US National Archives.

[2] In 1957 the British Prime Minister, Harold Macmillan made an optimistic speech to a Conservative Rally in Bedford where he made his famous statement that "most of our people had never had it so good".

Cold War and the threat of nuclear annihilation loomed over the world for the next 50 years. Resources had to be redirected to defence and restrictions placed on liberty in order, it was said, to provide security. The end of the Cold War, however, did not see restoration of liberties in fact it got worse as a new 'threat' loomed in the form of 'terrorism' needing increased surveillance and people control, or so we were told again.

It is not within the scope of this book to delve into the causes of the Cold War, but it is the opinion of this writer that the Cold War led to the corporatist dominated world we live in today. And who can tell whether terrorism would be so threatening if interference in other nations's affairs had not been such a preoccupation of Western Governments over the decades following the end of confrontation with the Soviet Union.

But to understand this we need to examine why it was that the USA, Britain and other Western allies fell out so calamitously with the Soviet Union (USSR), who together had worked so successfully to defeat Germany and its allies. Was the Cold War solely the fault of the USSR and the peddling of its communistic dogma which was anathema to many in the West, or were there other forces at work?

It is well known that the end of the war saw a scramble for German rocket scientists and military intelligence officers. But what interests us here is that some in Corporate America and former German intelligence assets had a common interest in the destruction, or at least neutering, of their former eastern comrades in arms.

It is not so well known that Germany's most senior military intelligence officer on the eastern war front, Major General Reinhard Gehlen, had a particular need to avoid falling into the hands of the Soviets in 1945. Gehlen, a specialist on the Soviets, derived much of his expertise from his role in one of the most terrible atrocities of the war: the torture, interrogation, and murder by starvation, of some 4 million Soviet prisoners of war[3].

---

[3] Christopher Simpson's book Blowback – Collier / Macmillan 1988.

Gehlen and his top aides willingly surrendered to American counter intelligence on 22nd May 1945. The Americans, who regarded them as a potential asset in the confrontation with USSR and Communism, freed them before the end of the year. They were installed in a former Waffen SS training facility in Germany.

'Gehlen's impact on the course of the Cold War', writes Christopher Simpson in his book 'Blowback', 'was subtle, but real', and those who opposed the questionable employment of Gehlen and former Nazis were overruled on pragmatic grounds. Allen Dulles[4], corporate lawyer, banker, director of the Council on Foreign Relations (CFR), future director of the CIA, and wartime Chief of the Office of Strategic Studies (OSS) in Berne under Major General Bill Donavan, argued: "He's on our side, and that's all that matters".

Prof Cutter in his study of Allen Dulles and his activities during the Cold War, writes: 'General Reinhard Gehlen's Organisation[5], the German equivalent of the CIA, falsified threats from encroaching communism to the extent that the polarization of global meridians in the Cold War reached the level of an atomic planetary holocaust in the 1962 Cuban missile blockade crisis'.

Christopher Simpson[6] continues in 'Blowback': 'Gehlen's reports and analyses [on the Soviet Union] were sometimes simply retyped onto CIA stationery and presented to President Truman without further comment', adding 'Gehlen's organisation "shaped what we knew about the Soviets in Eastern Europe"'. The German magazine Der Speigel asserted that 'seventy percent of all the US Government's information on Soviet forces and armaments came from the Gehlen organisation'.

Whether the Soviet Union was as big a threat to the West as was

---

[4] See : 'Architects of the Cold War' by Prof. Paul S. Cutter.

[5] Known simply as 'the Org' in intelligence circles.

[6] Chrisopher Simpson, professor of journalism and author, known internationally for his expertise in propaganda, democracy and media theory and practice.

portrayed or not, the Soviets following WWII must themselves have felt threatened. With the early American monopoly of nuclear weapons and a demonstrated willingness to use them, an initial lead in rocket technology through the employment of Nazi rocket scientists and the massive and successful anti-Soviet propaganda campaign waged by the West in general and the US in particular through the absorption of Gehlen's fabricated intelligence, the question remains who was largely responsible for the Cold War?

To be sure the USSR and its communist ideology was a threat to Corporate America. So it's not surprising that the American corporate sector, its agents and the American military industrial complex became so active after 1945. They must, though, take their share of blame for the advent and continuation of the Cold War (no attempt seems to have been made in the early days to enter into dialogue with the USSR to put a halt to the developing confrontation). That the Soviets responded is therefore understandable, but we will never know whether the West would have faced the belligerence it did if the ingredients from the American side had not been present in the first place.

The fear at the time was palpable.[7]

As frequently happens, fear is employed by governments and the establishment to manipulate public opinion into supporting particular political objectives – we are encouraged to give up a little of our freedom and democratic rights in exchange for security[8].

The stalwarts, especially in the European Movement, pushing for European integration, used the Soviet 'threat' during the Cold War years as justification for urging nations to 'share their sovereignty' (euphemism for abandoning liberties and democratic rights for the so called, greater good).

In retrospect, we can see much of the advance in democratic rights

---

[7] This writer recalls, as a 9 year old, asking his mother if the Russians (as they were still called at the time) were going to 'come and get us'.

[8] Benjamin Franklin in 1755, warned against this, stating: "Those who would give up essential liberty to purchase a little temporary safety, deserve neither liberty nor safety".

and freedoms gained in 19th century Britain through various parliamentary reforms, has been rolled back almost seamlessly in recent years. A stream of legislation has been enacted which eroded progress made, replacing beneficial government instead with a 'top down' system of control. Now government seems uncaring, remote and unaccountable – bureaucratic, rather than democratic[9]. And in recent years, a new dimension to the increasing feelings of subjugation has arisen through technological advances in surveillance techniques. And although supposedly for our own good to protect us from our enemies and criminality, surveillance has been increasingly used to spy upon the nations' own citizens.

This writer believes like many people, that:

'Power springs, or ought to spring, from the people.'

But when Prime Minister David Cameron returned from the World Economic Forum's annual meeting at Davos in January 2012, he declared that "we must stop knocking the bankers". Not an unsurprising statement considering 80% of Conservative Party funding was at the time reported as deriving from those same bankers.

Sadly, giant corporations, through their political acolytes, now rule the world. But once, for a while in Britain, things were different. Through the ideas of people like Thomas Paine, the efforts of other reformers, and sometimes the spilling of blood, the First Reform Act[10] and subsequent acts led to the extension of the franchise until all adults over the age of 18 were entitled to the vote.

Enfranchisement was, however, bitterly resisted by the ruling class of the time; the Prime Minister of the day, the Duke of Wellington, who had previously earned fame leading the British and Allied Armies to victory during the Napoleonic Wars, strongly opposed

---

[9] We are told that it's the 'New World Order', Globalisation. Complaint, whether about over-bearing development planning approvals, or inequitable treatment by local government are met by fatuous or no replies. There seems to be no recourse to grievances, petitions and appeals are generally ignored .

[10] Representation of the People Act, 1832

these measures[11].

In the 1860s, Walter Bagehot, son of a West Country banking family wrote: 'The English Constitution'. Bagehot, ignoring the fact that the executive is accountable to the rule of law (meaning in this instance the Constitution), promulgated the idea that it is parliament, through the bills it passes, that make the constitution, writing:

'The ultimate authority in the English Constitution is a newly elected House of Commons'.

This was an assertion contradicting the Declaration and Bill of Rights (1689), the Coronation Oath, The Act of Settlement and diametrically opposed to the ideas of the 18th century political philosopher Thomas Paine, who wrote[12]:

'[G]overnment has no right to make itself a party in any debate respecting the principles or modes of forming, or of changing, constitutions. It is not for the benefit of those who exercise the powers of government, that constitutions, and the governments issuing from them, are established.'

This, of course, is commonsense eloquently expressed.

It is not surprising that Thomas Paine[13] is ignored and not taught in schools. Thomas Paine is anathema to the ruling elite, the ideas of Walter Bagehot being preferred[14]. Bagehot believed that only the higher orders should rule:

'The lower orders, the middle orders, are still when tried by what is the standard of the educated 'ten thousand', narrow minded, unintelligent and incurious.'

and:

---

[11] When a national railway was being rolled out, Wellington objected, saying that it would encourage people to move about.

[12] Rights of Man, 1792 publication, Part III, Chapter III, page 32.

[13] Tom Paine, A political life, John Keane, Bloomsbury.

[14] The British Constitution in the 20th Century by Vernon Bogdanor (British Academy Centenary Monograph); The Constitution of the United Kingdom by Peter Leyland (Hart Publishing) are publications in the same vein as Bagehot's 'English Constitution'.

'Hobbes[15] told us long ago, and everybody now understands that there must be a supreme authority, a conclusive power in every state on every point somewhere. The idea of government involves it — when that idea is properly understood.'

That Bagehot's book[16], essentially a reaction to the First Reform Act of 1832 and the 'threat' of the proposed 1867 Second Reform Act extending the franchise. That the book should be held in such high regard by politicians is perhaps a measure of how far they are removed from the idea of what constitutes a democracy.

It's also a measure of the ignorance at large, that the government in general and the Prime Minister David Cameron in particular, are presently busy putting together a Bill of Rights[17] totally ignoring the fact we already have one[18] that fits the 'Thomas Paine test' (see above) — a Constitution that is essentially derived from the concept that all people should have a say in how they are governed and taxed. It is a written, but uncodified, Constitution consisting primarily of the Magna Carta, The Grand Remonstrance 1641, Declaration and Bill of Rights (1688(9) and the Coronation Oath.

The Declaration and Bill of Rights came about as a result of James II's authoritarian rule and his belief in the 'Divine Right of Kings', particularly Stuart Kings. James fled the country when it seemed he was about to be overthrown and William of Orange was then conditionally offered the Crown. He was required to agree to the Declaration of Rights which was later enacted by Parliament as the Bill of Rights. The Declaration, a constitutional document, limited the powers of the Crown, yet politicians today see the resulting Bill of Rights as giving parliament carte blanche to do as they please,

---

15 Thomas Hobbes in his 'The Leviathan (a word derived from Hebrew meaning "sea monster")' argues the state of nature is the "war of every man against every man," in which people constantly seek to destroy one another. This state is so horrible that human beings naturally seek peace, and the best way to achieve peace is to construct the Leviathan through social contract.
16 Available from the Houses of Parliament bookshop, Parliament Square; and is said to be required reading for all new MPs.
17 'From the Human Rights Act to a Bill of Rights?', Parliament web-site: www:parliament.uk
18 'Unlawful Governance' and 'Understanding a written part of our Constitution — The Coronation Oath, The Declaration and Bill of Rights 1688(9)', by John Bingley.

even to the extent of the old adage, sometimes taught to schoolchildren, that parliament could legislate that 'all new born blue-eyed children should be put to death', if they wanted to. This, besides being patently absurd, is also contrary to the Constitution[19] which prohibits cruel and unusual punishments.

But anyone visiting the Parliament Bookshop in Parliament Square London will find copies of Bagehot and similar tomes on sale and any attempt to have them stock what is considered to be the real Constitution will not be entertained. Bagehot is required reading for new MPs and they will then tell you:

'The British Constitution consists of eight words[20], *'what the Queen enacts in Parliament is law'*. David Cameron further claimed: *'So parliament can pass any EU treaty or constitution into law, or repeal it'*. This, then, is what they mean by the *'Sovereignty of Parliament'*.

But Pitt the Elder, referring to the Bill of Rights 1688(9), said:

"*..... instead of the arbitrary power of a King* [referring to James II], *we must submit to the arbitrary power of a House of Commons? If this be true, what benefit do we have from the exchange? Tyranny, my lords, is detestable in every shape, but in none so formidable as when it is assumed and exercised by a number of tyrants. But this is not the fact; this is not the Constitution. We have a law of Parliament. We have a code in which every honest man may find it. We have the Magna Charta. We have the Statute Book, and the Bill of Rights*".

This is an accurate understanding of the Bill of Rights. The 'Queen in Parliament' is subject to the rule of law meaning that parliament is subject to the Constitution[21]. Now that the role of the monarch and the House of Lords (Parliament Act 1911) has been subsumed, it is even more important that the public are protected from

---

[19] Bill of Rights 1688(9).

[20] Email David Cameron to this writer in 2001.

[21] In response to a question by MP, Tony Benn in July 1993, the speaker of the House of Commons, Betty Boothroyd, confirmed the status of the Bill of Rights when she said that the 1689 Bill of Rights provided that freedom of speech in Parliament "ought not to be questioned in any place out of Parliament".

arbitrary rule by enforcement of the Constitution.

The public elect MPs for a parliament, 'lending' them powers to legislate for a period up to five years. At the end of that period the powers are returned to the people who decide in an election whom next to lend them to. By handing powers to an unelected European Union executive, Parliament has broken this convention and also contravened the Bill of Rights:

' ..... *noe Forreigne Prince Person Prelate, State or Potentate hath or ought to have any Jurisdiction Power Superiority Preeminence or Authoritie Ecclesiasticall or Spirituall within this Realme Soe helpe me God.'*

But now giant corporations, through the politicians they bank-roll, and through extra-national institutions such as the World Economic Forum at Davos and the European Union have almost imperceptibly taken a huge role in the decision making process. How can power ever spring from the people in these circumstances?[22]

This book has been adapted from the CD produced by this writer in 2006, entitled 'Shoe-horned into the EU' and covers the period 1970-1972. It tells the story of the shenanigans of Prime Minister Edward Heath and his Government aided and abetted by the European Movement and a corrupted, unscrupulous Civil Service (essentially the Foreign and Commonwealth Office) to deceive parliament and the people into joining what was portrayed as a trading block (the EEC). But in reality it was a first step in a series of treaties that has taken us into an unelected, unaccountable and corporate influenced bureaucracy, whilst at the same time, inevitably, undermining national democratic processes.

In 1970, the people elected Edward Heath's Conservative Party to govern for the people. But instead, Heath abdicated his responsibilities and knowingly began the process of handing power to giant corporations and global bankers, who through the EU's

---

[22] Peter Mandleson, during his tenure as an EU commissioner, in a speech in Bonn, Germany, in March 1998, claimed: *'The age of true representative democracy is now coming to an end* – from Tony Benn's book: 'A political life'.

Brussels' bureaucratic system, increasingly exercise this power. National sovereign power has ebbed away through a series of treaties, to such an extent that ordinary working people now have to compete with job seekers from Eastern Europe who are prepared to work for knock-down wages[23]. The resulting fall in wages suit corporate interests whose control of policies brought them about in the first place.

This loss of sovereign power is partly explained in Dr Peter Gardner's book: 'A Hard Pounding'[24] which puts it down to a loss of will, and weakness of government following the 1956 Suez debacle. There was also fear that Britain could not compete against a resurgent Germany which had, it was said, gained from hidden assets acquired during WWII and from American aide through the Marshall Plan. This is not to deny, of course, a national propensity for hard work and ingenuity.

There was another more insidious cause (to this collective loss of morale); the loss of Empire was hard to bear for those who once held sway over one third of the globe. These elites saw, in the European Union, a substitute 'empire'[25]. John Stevens, leader of the Pro-EU Conservative Party, at a debate in 2001 in Shipton-under-Wychwood where PM David Cameron[26] was a participant, proudly proclaiming that "the EU would, one day, become a new empire".

There were others with a more honourable, but dangerously naïve belief in European integration. They held that a European Union would end wars – a contention hard to sustain in 2014.

---

23 Freedom of movement directive.

24 Re-published by this writer in 2014.

25 Geoffrey Tucker, Heath's coordinator of the public propaganda campaign from 1970 -72, a convert to European integration, said, following the 1956 Suez debacle, "I've been converted to being a pro-European as against believing in the Empire".

26 Yet in the following decade Cameron as PM, would be echoing the same sort of language with his declaration that he wished to see "Europe stretching from the Atlantic to the Urals" – Booker Column, 20th December 2014.

Meanwhile the major driving force behind the abolition of nation states and their sub-summation into a 'Greater Europe' is a growing global corporate sector whose wealth sometimes exceeds the GDP of whole countries. Their influence and control is assisted through a myriad of international bodies remote from the democratic process.

It is in this context that 'Shoe-horned into the EU' has been adapted and augmented to show how an elected government used grossly unfair and deceitful methods, corporate money, corporate media and a corporate supported European Movement, to begin the process of depriving the people of Britain the power to make their own laws and the consequences that have followed.

PART I

Prime Minister Edward Heath's
Campaign to take Britain into the EEC

(in collaboration with the European
Movement)

18th June 1970 - 1st January 1973

FOLLOW THE MONEY

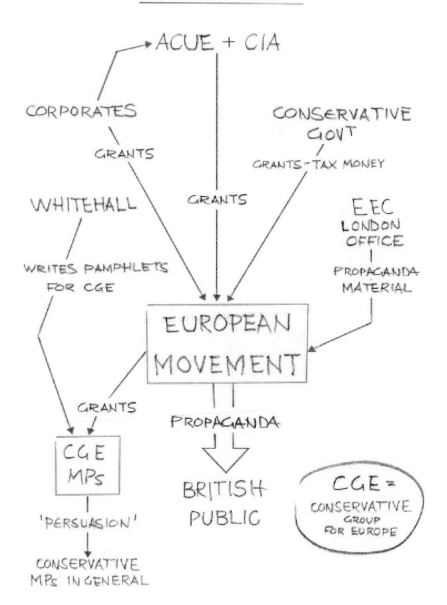

CHAPTER 1

No loss of essential National Sovereignty

The Government White Paper on the failed 'Treaty establishing a Constitution for Europe', issued in September 2004, stated that:

'By the time the UK joined the EEC in 1973, the principle of primacy (that European law takes precedence over national law) was also firmly established.'

Yet the Chancellor of the Duchy of Lancaster, Geoffrey Rippon, moving the motion on the 15th February 1972[1], for the Second Reading of the Bill which took us into the EEC, said: *"there would be no essential surrender of sovereignty..."*.

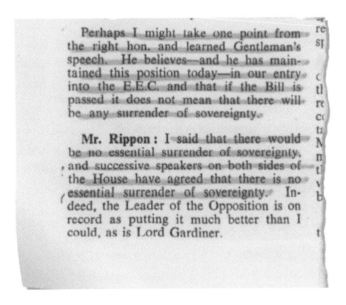

Perhaps I might take one point from the right hon. and learned Gentleman's speech. He believes—and he has maintained this position today—in our entry into the E.E.C. and that if the Bill is passed it does not mean that there will be any surrender of sovereignty.

Mr. Rippon: I said that there would be no essential surrender of sovereignty, and successive speakers on both sides of the House have agreed that there is no essential surrender of sovereignty. Indeed, the Leader of the Opposition is on record as putting it much better than I could, as is Lord Gardiner.

This mantra, in one form or another, was repeated throughout the campaign and the debates in Parliament. So either the author(s) of the White Paper had a poor grasp of the facts, or were deliberately setting out to mislead and misinform Parliament and the public, in 2004.

---

[1] Hansard.

It is typical of the contradiction between what Parliament and the public were told in the period leading up to the Parliamentary votes on the European Communities Act 1972 (ECA72) and the reality of what joining meant for British sovereignty. FCO 30/1048 demonstrate clearly that the effect on national sovereignty was well known by the Government and its officials dealing with the issue. This awareness is also proven by the correspondence and reports from the Foreign and Commonwealth Office (FCO) described in the following chapters[1].

FCO 30/1048 and David Noakes' commentary (refer to Part II, Chapter.4 of this book) is important for an understanding of the deception perpetrated on the British public. For example; we read in paragraph 26:

'*To control and supervise this process* [i.e. officials and negotiators are to assume political roles] *it will be necessary to strengthen the democratic organisation of the Community with consequent decline of the primacy and prestige of the national parliaments*'.

'*The task will not be to arrest this process, since to do so would be to put considerations of formal sovereignty before effective influence and power, but to adapt institutions and policies both in the UK and in Brussels to meet and reduce the real and substantial public anxieties over national identity and alienation from government, fear of change and loss of control over their fate which are aroused by talk of the "loss of sovereignty"*'.

Dr Richard North, who has also studied and reported on FCO 30/1048, described his feelings about paragraph.26, in his paper entitled '*Sovereignty and the European Communities*', dated 17th February 2002: '*... and chillingly, these civil servants applaud the process. They 'know' [knew] what they have [had] to do*'.

Other examples of the Heath Government's, and in particular, the FCO's concealment of important knowledge they had of the implications for sovereignty and the Constitution of joining the

---

[1] This book, whilst providing a large number of extracts from correspondence and documentation from the time, is no substitute for examining the almost comprehensive archive of material in the CD: 'Shoe-horned into the EU', available additionally to those purchasing this book.

EEC, is on record in the internal memos of the time. For instance a memo from W.J. Adams, Head of the European Communities Information Unit (ECIU) to a Mr Morland, of the European Information Department (EID), demonstrated the wish to keep the true situation from becoming widely known: '...*be aware of the Conservative Group for Europe's wish to play down this issue as far as possible and reassure those people in parliament and in the country who get emotional about loss of sovereignty*'.

We shall see more of Mr Adams contempt for democracy and for the public that he was supposed to serve later in this account.

It may be legal (this aspect is the subject of debate), but is it possible for it to be claimed that our membership of the EU has legitimacy and that the EU has the right to govern those millions within its domain?

CHAPTER 2

Heath's Campaign 1970 - 1972

Edward Heath had always been an ardent integrationist and in the early 1960s he was appointed by Harold Macmillan to pursue negotiations with the EEC with a view to Britain joining the other six members. The attempt foundered in February 1963 with the President of France, General de Gaulle's veto.

Heath subsequently became the leader of the Conservative opposition in parliament and was leader at the time of the 1970 General Election. He was adamant that Britain's place was at the 'Heart of Europe' and campaigned in the election against a background of public hostility to entry. Polls of the time showed 70% of the people against, with only 18% in favour. Then, as now, there was deep distrust of the idea. People were quite happy with the way they were governed, after all they had a say in it.

To address this, Heath set out to provide the public with reassurance and comfort. Just before the 1970 General Election, he made a key-note speech in Paris on 5th May 1971 to the British Chamber of Commerce, repeating his message during the election campaigning with a promise that he would *"not go in"* without *"the full-hearted consent of Parliament and the people"*.

Heath unexpectedly[1] won the 18th June General Election with a small majority of just 30 seats[2], but with the benefit, apparently, of a 'purchased' copy of the Labour Party's election, plans[3] for

---

[1] Heath won despite being 12 points behind in the weeks before the election.

[2] One can speculate as to whether Heath would have gained a majority had he been honest about his intentions and the fact he knew that it was not just a 'Common Market' he was proposing to join.

[3] The story of how the Conservative Party acquired details of Harold Wilson's election strategy was related by Geoffrey Tucker, Heath's Communications Director, in a confession shortly before he died. Tucker admitted that he paid a Labour Part official to sell him the plans. This account was reported in the Mail on Sunday's 19th January 2003's edition (this author retains a copy of the newspaper article). More details are provided on Page.16, in a footnote to William Whitelaw, Chief Whip at the time, who apparently approved the deal when the Party Chairman, Anthony Barber, refused to do so..

£25,000. This unorthodox electioneering ploy set the scene for the following two years' of Heath Government. He immediately set to work to persuade the public that they must join the EEC. Use of the words 'lying and deceit' should be reserved for the rarest of occasions, but it is up to the reader to decide whether this description fits after reading this exposé.

The Players

The main players in this blessed plot (to use the title of Hugo Young's book reviewing membership of the EU) to shoe-horn Britain in at any cost were:

For the Government:

The BBC.

Other visual media including ITV (there was no Sky News in those days).

The Press (most of the press).

Jean Monnet and his Action Committee for a United States of Europe.

The European Movement (sometimes mutating into 'Britain in Europe' for specific campaigns). A leading player was Ernest Wistrich. Wistrich and the European Movement were welcomed by government almost as if a department of state, playing a vital role during the propaganda campaign.

The Foreign and Commonwealth Office (FCO) and particularly its Information Research Department (IRD) led by Norman Reddaway (Assistant Under Secretary for Information at the FCO).

Other sub-units of the FCO involved, included the European Integration Department (EID) led by Mr Statham, the European Communities Information Unit (ECIU), headed by W J Adams – acting as a sort of information controller. Conservative Party Group for Europe (CGE). Conservative Ministers and many MPs. Lord President of the Council, William Whitelaw appointed by Heath to organise and conduct the Government campaign. Whitelaw was also leader of the House of Commons; he carried out his task with dedication.

CBI[4], with Michael King its Information Officer.

Covert participation of the EEC's Brussels' office in London

For the opposition:

The under-funded (no government money being provided) 'Keep Britain Out' campaign, led by Christopher Frere-Smith.

Morning Star newspaper.

Peter Shore

Individual MPs acting alone or in collaboration:

Enoch Powell MP, Peter Shore MP, Tony Benn MP, Douglas Jay MP, father of Peter Jay, presenter of the BBC's Money Programme into the 1990s.

The Public Campaign

There was little time to be wasted. Heath's majority was small and the British economy in poor shape, with high unemployment, rising inflation and trouble from militant unions – the Heath Government might fall at any time. The Bill

Douglas Jay

Picture kindly provided by his son, Peter Jay

for accession to the EEC was to have its First Reading in October 1971, just 15 months away, and there was much to be done.

Ministers decided in late May 1971 following negotiations between Prime Minister Edward Heath and President Pompidou of France in Paris and the Chancellor of the Duchy of Lancaster, Geoffrey Rippon in Brussels, that they had '*to convince members of Parliament that the tide of public opinion was moving in their favour*'[5]. Those were

---

[4] Confederation of British Industry.

[5] FCO 26/1215, Appendix II, Page.6, 'Approach to Europe', 15th February 1972, written by

the days when MPs were more attuned to constituent's views.

It is one of the objectives of Part II of this book, to show that the methods employed by Heath's Government, perhaps more than anything else, precipitated the cynical attitude of people to politics and politicians current today. Heath and his cohorts were not opposed to accepting money from those with vested interests (corporations) in a Federal Europe and not bothered by questions of the morality of employing deception to turn public opinion and Parliament to their way of thinking.

The fact that the records of the campaign were classified 'confidential' or 'SECRET' and hidden away from public gaze for 30 years (under the '30 Year Rule') demonstrates the regime was sensitive to a possible public backlash should the truth emerge. A backlash could have impacted upon the future course of the development of Britain's relations with the expanding federal superstate across the Channel.

Anthony Royle, later Lord Fanshaw, as a record of the Government's campaign and intended to be used as a 'guide for possible future information campaigns'.

CHAPTER 3

The Civil Service in action

The audio track[1], '*A Letter to the Times*', highlights perhaps better than ten thousand words, the work of the FCO's Information Research Department (IRD) led by Norman Reddaway (pictured right). Reddaway had been an IRD, MI5/6 operative in the destabilisation of Indonesian President Sukarno in the 1960s. The department had its origins in the Special Operations Executive (SOE) in the Second World War. So IRD[2] had a good pedigree when it came to subversion and it was, sadly, only too willing to use its skills on the home front to assist in the process of subsuming an unwilling people into the orbit of unaccountable European bureaucracy.

Norman Reddawav

Geoffrey Tucker[3], prominent on the audio track was an advertising guru and Heath's coordinator of the public propaganda campaign. Tucker was the man interfacing between the EEC negotiating team in Brussels, the European Movement (partly Government-funded[4]), IRD/FCO/MI5/MI6 (Norman Reddaway), the press and the visual media. In other words, he had an important influence upon campaign strategy.

It is perhaps remarkable that Heath could so soon after winning the 1970 election mobilise and mould the civil service so speedily to

---

[1] Can be accessed on the CD: 'Shoe horned into the EU', available from the author.

[2] According to a Guardian article of 26th August 2006, a department called RICU (Research, Information and Communication Unit), was set up in 2005 by the then Home Secretary, John Reid, 'to exploit new media websites and outlets with a proposal to "channel messages through volunteers in internet forums"' – sounds like it may be a more advanced successor to IRD but immersing itself in the public domain to influence public attitudes and opinion.

[3] See footnote.3, Chapter.2. And footnote 11 this Chapter regarding Labour mole providing 1970 general election plans.

[4] Whilst the Conservative Government and CIA were funding the European Movement, the European Movement were passing on some of these funds to the Conservative Group for Europe (CGE). They received £4524 from the EM in the critical period 1971-2 and £18,000 in 1973 according to 'The Conservative Europeanist' authored by N.J. Crowson.

his will and find so many willing hands to participate in, to use Hugo Young's phrase again, '*this blessed plot*'.

At regular private breakfast meetings, known as the 'Breakfast Club', a programme of action was agreed to including orchestrating letters to the Times and other newspapers. They were written by FCO officials for willing MPs to put their signatures to[5]. The meetings were held in the luxury Connaught Hotel, in London's Mayfair. These breakfasts took place weekly throughout most of the campaign.

The breakfasts were clearly central to coordinating the public campaign, allowing Government ministers and officials to meet journalists and media people secretly, 'away from prying eyes'. Indeed, they had much to hide and those taking part, if they were still alive today, would be most perturbed to learn that their participation is now public knowledge. Roy Hattersley, a one-time Labour Government minister and one of those still living at the time of writing this book, was so disgusted at the 'conniving' outside of normal governmental practices that, to his credit, he never attended again after his first and only meeting.

Those attending included[6], besides Geoffrey Tucker and Mr Garret, his official coordinator, the head and director of public relations at Conservative Central Office; Ernest Wistrich (Director of the European Movement); Anthony Royle (Ministerial coordinator); Geoffrey Rippon, Chancellor of the Duchy of Lancaster (Chief

between Mr. Tucker and the official op of chairman, those who attended from time to time included other members of the Standing Group and, each in his personal capacity: the Prime Minister's political Secretary, the Editor of the Economist, the Managing Director ITN, the Managing Director BBC Radio, the Head of Current Affairs BBC TV, the Secretary of Aims for Industry, the Secretary of the

Post ECA(72) First Reading Campaign Report by Anthony Royle

---

[5] MPs were often quite happy to oblige as it provided an opportunity to get their names into print (quote by Geoffrey Tucker on 'Letter to the Times' track).

[6] Report 'Approach to Europe' by Anthony Royle, FCO 26/1215.

negotiator in Brussels); Heath's political secretary at No.10 Downing Street (Douglas Hurd MP, now Lord Hurd of Westwell); the editor of the Economist[7]; the Managing Director of ITN; the Managing Director of BBC Radio, Ian Trethowen; the Head of Current Affairs BBC TV; the Secretary of State for Aims of Industry; the Secretary of the Industrial Policy Group, a Director of ORC; the Liberal Chief Whip; the Secretary of the Labour Committee for Europe; the Assistant General Secretary of the Labour Party and personal assistant to Roy Jenkins.

The book, 'Britain's Secret Propaganda War'[8], (page 148) states that people from the Brussels establishment also attended:

'Into the breakfasts came the people from Brussels'.

These constituted a veritable roll-call of the great and the good.

It is noticeable that Roy Hattersley's name has been left off Anthony Royle's list (see footnote above). He wisely placed himself outside the conspiracy as previously mentioned.

Geoffrey Tucker explained (as recorded) in '*Letter to the Times*' that he kept a notebook with three important headings:

1. Objective:

'To convince MPs that the tide of public opinion is moving towards joining the EEC'.

2. Method:

'We must rely greatly on the fast media':

TV – News at 10, 24 Hours, Panorama

Radio – World at One, Today, Woman's Hour

Marshall Stewart, then editor of the Today programme, cooperated fully with the Breakfast Club meetings and may even have been one of the TV people present. In any case, we are told, the collaborators succeeded in getting an extra five minutes added to the Today

---

[7] Today the Economist is partly owned by Rothschilds. Position in 1970s unknown.
[8] By Paul Lashmar and James Oliver.

Programme to broadcast pro-EEC propaganda.

3. Nobbling:

"Nobbling is the name of the game", said Tucker. "This involved direct day-by-day communications between our people and media personnel; e.g. FCO and Marshall Stewart of the Today Programme".

A major problem for the Government was that some of the media presenters were unsympathetic to the 'project' and they decided that they had to be removed (i.e. no serious opposition was to be brooked).

The net result of 'nobbling' and propaganda was that a sceptical public who were only 18% in favour of joining the Common Market (EEC) with 70% against in December 1970, were for a short critical period in July 1971 evenly balanced (51:49) for entry. This, together with other pressures (see later) on MPs, was sufficient to persuade parliamentarians to vote at the First Reading of ECA(72) on 28th October 1971 for the motion – to join the EEC at least in principle.

The Foreign and Commonwealth Office (FCO)

Documentation, released to the public under the '30 year rule[9]', reveals seven FCO departments were involved in the campaign[10]:

1. The Information Research Department (IRD) referred to above and headed by Norman Reddaway, was the lead department in the campaign. This department was involved more than any other in the propaganda and disinformation effort and also set out to undermine those struggling to oppose the Government's programme. It is clear from the documentation that Reddaway was quite ruthless about how he utilized the civil service to misrepresent the case for joining and to neutralise opposition.

In a memo of 30th September 1970, just three months after the

---

[9] National Archives, Kew, available on CD: 'Shoe-horned into EU', copy available from this author.

[10] We have no idea how they coped with their regular work load.

General Election, he wrote: '*The discreet promotion of letters to the press through confidential brokers should now sharply increase*......' and a few lines later in the memo: '*BCEM* [European Movement] *liaison is likewise important*'. There is much in the same vein accessible through the the CD, available to readers.

Reddaway is not reticent in using 'Goebbelic' style conditioning on

my Minute o. .. . . Secretary of State would welcome additional suggestions.

2.   We have now made a useful start on discreet support for the approach to Europe. Mr Budd's liaison with publicists, Mr Tyrer's list of pro and anti-marketeers, Mr Tucker's work on the HMSO booklet and the Speaking Notes, Miss Waller's approach to women's organisations and Mr Hill's talks with COI over T.V. possibilities are all useful. Three suggestions additional to those in my Minute of 17 September:

    (a)   The discreet promotion of letters to the press through confidential brokers should now sharply increase, as suggested by Mr Royle (paragraph 5). Arrangements are being made by Mr Budd and Mr Tucker.

    (b)   Pro-marketeers could be helped by discreet use of IAD Visits Section. By consulting Mr Budd and Mr Tyrer's list, IAD can d~.. .. ~-lpful lists for entertainments

his own countrymen. In his memo entitled 'THE MESSAGE' dated 10th September 1970, he writes: '*The message should be coherent and simple. Repetition is essential*'.

'THE MESSAGE' (four pages) is an illuminating document demonstrating that the art of spin preceded Alistair Campbell by several decades. Reddaway had worked out his own ideas about the benefits of membership. Whether or not he believed his own propaganda we shall never know. One suspects that, being an experienced and dedicated professional, he enjoyed this sort of work for its own sake. The desire for truth and balance may not have mattered much to him.

IRD's work output for the public campaign was quite prolific. They:

— wrote over 50 articles for national and regional newspapers

— wrote pamphlets for the Conservative Group for Europe (CGE), a group financed by the European Movement, in turn financed by corporate business, the CIA and, quite inexcusably, the Conservative Government itself using (or misusing taxpayer's money)

— kept a steady stream of letters and articles to the press from September 1970 until October 1971

— drafted replies to over 2000 letters from the general public

SECRET

15. Between September 1970 and October 1971 IRD kept up a steady stream of letters and articles to the Press, working closely with the European Movement, and also drafted the replies to over 2,000 letters from the general public.

ACTIVITIES IN SCHOOLS

17. The European Movement commissioned Education Productions Limited to produce a series of wall charts on Britain and the EEC for use in schools. Occasional schools conferences were arranged and the European Movement provided speakers for school talks.

RESEARCH SUPPORT

— prepared about 60 separate background briefs for speakers, journalists and politicians, in addition to providing general reference material and speaking notes

2. The European Information Department (EID) drafted speeches and letters. They even drafted a speech for Denis Howell MP[11] for the Labour Party conference. The reader may wonder what a government department was doing writing party speeches, but this was a regular sort of activity throughout the campaign.

---

[11] Denis Howell, MP for Birmingham constituencies, went on to become the EEC Commissioner for Regional Policy. He was later honoured with the title Lord Howell of Aston Manor.

3. The European Communities Information Unit (ECIU) planned the 'Information Effort in the UK' as well as the 'Information Effort

> about the latter.
>
> (c) There should also be a panel of less well-known speakers capable of addressing Women's Institutes, Rotary Clubs, etc. The programme for such speakers should concentrate on constituencies represented by M.P.'s who were doubtful about entry: there was no need to worry about those where the Member was already in favour.
>
> (d) We should get together a team of writers able to work e.g.
>   ... The ... two or those ...
>
> (e) An exercise must be mounted to ensure a constant stream of good Supplementary Questions on the E.E.C. in the House of Commons. Sir A. Meyer might be able to help with this.
>
> (f) A campaign of letter-writing to M.P.'s by constituents must also be promoted.
>
> 3. Mr. Royle made the general point that speeches about the E.E.C.

overseas'. They also seem to have had a role in intelligence gathering, in particular, seeking out those people who were for and against, so that action could be taken to enlist their support for the campaign or neutralise those thought likely to give trouble. For instance, they carried out an operation on BBC Scotland determining that '*All those involved in News and Current Affairs are pro-Marketeers and we can depend upon them to press for as much time as possible*'[12]. So much for civil service impartiality.

Also in the same letter ECIU writes: '*I have written to the regional organiser of the European Movement in Edinburgh ......*'. This was an important operation for the FCO, because opinion was much more firmly set against entry in Scotland then, than the rest of the country.

Another ECIU letter shows the unit organising speakers for recalcitrant MP's constituencies in order to put pressure on them through their constituents – hardly a proper role for a public servant[13]: '*A campaign of letter writing to MPs by constituents must also*

---

[12] Letter from S.A. Budd dated 9th September 1971 to Mr Adams and Mr Hugh Jones.

[13] An example of the intimidation elected representatives faced is shown in Part II of this book, where Neil Marten, MP for Banbury, campaigner against the bill - ECA72 , was given special attention. This was done, not so much to make him change his mind, but to attempt to divert him from his campaigning efforts.

helpful and pro........ ....etary:)

3. On (h), there is no problem at all with BBC TV Scotland. All of those involved in News and Current Affairs are pro-Marketeers and we can depend upon them to press for as much time as possible.

4. George Reid and Russell Galbraith of STV are both,

... Fleming .... the Reg......, ... I will soon his out on other plans).

5. I have written to the Regional Organiser of the European Movement in Edinburgh, telling him of Sir J Marjoribanks' forthcoming engagements, and no doubt he will do all he can to help out with publicity.

be promoted', shows the determination of the Government and its campaigners to take the public by storm and ensure it got what it wanted – transfer of the democratic rights to EEC sponsored corporatist forces.

The records continue: '*There was, in addition, regular contact between ECIU and the producers of major current affairs programmes*' where their help was needed to get the message out to the public. Civil service impartiality was not to be on the agenda.

4. Guidance and Information Policy (GIP)

The records refer to this unit in campaign correspondence, but fail to make clear how this branch of government was involved.

5. Information Administration Department (IAD)

This unit had the function of controlling the information output to the campaign, presumably to avoid inconsistency of message and to ensure maximum public impact. No doubt it was this department that suppressed FCO 30/1048[14] – the 1971 document that analysed the expected impact on sovereignty from joining the EEC.

IAD had '*substantial funds available for visits*' and used these to set up a dedicated Visits Section. They '*launched a major programme of 1000*

---

[14] Refer to Part.II, Chapter. 3.

visits a year from Western Europe. These visits were aimed at creating a favourable climate of opinion in Europe and, at the same time, helping to educate domestic opinion about Europe'.

6. Cultural Relations Department (CRD)

The records do not make clear the role of this department.

7. East/West Contacts and Student Welfare (EWCSW). This

VISITS

10.   The Visits Section of the FCO's Information Administration Department launched a major programme of 1,000 visits a year from Western Europe. These visits were aimed at creating a favourable climate of opinion in Europe and, at the same time, helping to educate domestic opinion about Europe. The FCO's annual grant of £7,500 to the European Movement for its own visits programme was topped up several times, and smaller donations were made to a number of other organisations. The EEC's

/London

department was responsible for the British Council, which was, itself, active in the campaign.

There were a number of other government departments involved in the campaign, indicating no expense was to be spared in achieving membership of the EEC.

Broadcast Media Participation

'Mr William Whitelaw[15], [President of the Council] said that he

---

[15] As we have seen in a footnote in the previous chapter, it was reported that William Whitelaw, Chief Whip at the time of the General Election, apparently gave approval for £25,000 to be paid to a Labour Party mole to provide the plans of the Labour Party's election tactics. The political editor, Simon Walters, of the Mail on Sunday who wrote the column dated 19th January 2003, claimed that 'if the bribe had been uncovered when Heath was Prime Minister between 1970 and 1974, it would almost have certainly led to him being forced out of office

would have a word with the BBC about a lack of co-operation on their part'. Willie Whitelaw, as he was affectionately known, was one of Mrs Thatcher's closest colleagues during the time of her administration?

> with television production at the Paddock
> that the Conservative Research Centre had a list of
> helpful businessmen which was confidential but could
> be made available to those attending the meeting. It
> was also decided that Mr. Michael King should be
> invited to Mr. Tucker's regular breakfasts as the
> linkman. Mr. Whitelaw said that he would have a word
> with the BBC about lack of co-operation on their part.
> 10. The meeting then discussed the problem of
> distribution of publicity material. Mr. Adams pointed

BBC QUASI GOVERNMENTAL

The actions of the press have been described elsewhere in this narrative. Here we are interested in how the broadcast media (TV and radio) rose to the challenge urged on them by the Government and the suggestion, resulting from Whitelaw's intended intervention, that the BBC was less independent and impartial than it declared itself to be.

William Whitelaw

Initially, TV and radio, particularly the BBC, we are told[16], were cool to the campaign, needing to maintain the impression of impartiality as required by their Charter. However, things changed rapidly under the onslaught from the FCO (in particular IRD) – no doubt as a result of the lead taken by William Whitelaw.

We are informed, in *'A letter to the Times'*: the *'flood of letters'* in the

---

and changed the course of British history. All those involved would have been sent to jail'. The Labour Party mole has never been identified [at the time of the revelation].

16 Anthony Royle's 'Approach to Europe' 1970/71, FCO26/1215, Appendix. II, pages.20/21.

press, written by IRD's officials and signed by MPs, 'induced a heightened interest'.

TV and radio executives, as we have seen, were invited to the weekly private strategic breakfasts discussions at the Connaught. The audio track, itself, speaks volumes regarding the altered stance of the BBC – it was Ian Trethowen, a friend of Heath, responding to pressure to remove '*anti-Europeans*', who got rid of Jack de Manio, the Radio 4 presenter, for being against joining the EEC.

That there may have been other removals or changes is indicated by Geoffrey Tucker, who reported:

"*we are fortunate that communicators were now basically in favour of our entry. This had not been true a few months ago*".

Royle recounted that Southern TV and Granada accepted assistance and Scottish TV accepted pressure to do more generally. He also reported that: '*Both television and radio, despite their rules of impartiality, were judged by the German Embassy, in a careful assessment in early August [1971], to be contributing importantly and favourably*'.

Royle concludes: '*The impact was immediate. Reports from all sources*

above). It produced the desired tide of public opinion in favour, at the right time, before MPs returned to their constituencies, and in particular before they entered the conference season in September. It did not succeed in the hope of sustaining public opinion right through, but it did succeed in achieving the targets of parity of public opinion by the Recess

indicated a substantial favourable movement of public opinion', and '*It produced the desired tide of public opinion in favour, at the right time before MPs returned to their constituencies, and in particular before they entered the conference season in September*'.

The power of TV is well know. That is why TV attracts massive fees from advertisers. This writer has been told by a retailer in his home town, that an advert for, say Mars bars, will show an immediate threefold increase in sales following a series of advertising broadcasts.

That the independent (by statute) broadcast media colluded in the

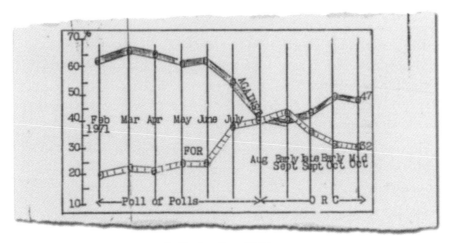

Poll of polls – 1971

Government's plan to deceive the public is a blot on that industry that remains to this day.

FCO Conspired to Neutralise the 'Keep Britain Out' campaign

Christopher Frere-Smith was the Chairman of the 'Keep Britain Out' campaign. The FCO took a dim view of the organisation's presence in the campaign and were disinterested in maintaining a level playing field, as internal memos and correspondence make clear.

For instance, Frere-Smith wrote to the FCO complaining of the lack of access to regulations and other instruments passed by the EEC, needed so as he could better inform the public of what joining meant, when campaigning.

A lowly official, Mr Simcock working in the EID, drafted a seemingly honest and satisfactory reply, listing the various locations where the documents could be viewed. He added, incorrectly though, that: *'the instruments will naturally be amended where necessary to take account of British interests before accession to the Community'*. Incorrectly, because the Government accepted a 'fait accompli', a take the whole of it, or leave it, situation.

The Government, desperate to get in this time, had singularly failed to negotiate the Treaty as promised in the Conservative Party election manifesto. This failure was the theme of a number of speeches during the Parliamentary debates as will be seen in the following pages.

However, W K Slatcher, Simcock's superior at EID, rejected his idea of cooperating with Frere-Smith, writing to his own manager, suggesting:

'In view of Mr Frere-Smith's notorious anti-market activities [Having a view about entry and campaigning for that view in a so called democratic society was now 'beyond the pale'], *it does not seem*

```
        I submit a draft reply for the Prime Minister's
signature to a letter from the Chairman of the Keep
Britain Out Campaign, complaining that Community
legislation is not available to the public.
2.    In view of Mr Frere-Smith's notorious anti-Market
activities, it does not seem incumbent upon us to tell
him the full story of the adaptation of secondary
legislation to British requirements nor of the
preparation of authentic English texts of Community
legislation.  The draft is therefore the least we can
say in rebuttal of his complaint.
3.    It has been cleared with the Librarian at the DTI.
```

CHAPTER 4

Jean Monnet and his Comité d'Action pour les États-Unis d'Europe

Jean Monnet, *éminence grise* and a supranationalist, operated behind-the-scenes, involving himself in every stage of the European 'project', until the 1970s. Contrary to the image projected in FCO documentation of Monnet as an avuncular figure interested only in progressing Britain's application for membership of the EEC, he was no friend of Britain.

He had worked to ensure that Britain was excluded from the European Coal and Steel Community in the early 1950s. This was about the time that the United States used its muscle to have the European Movement's Headquarters moved from London[1] to Brussels and Duncan Sandys replaced by Paul-Henri Spaak. The Americans at the same time, you will recall, had had funding transferred away from London. Monnet feared, correctly, Britain's involvement would interfere with his federalist plans.

By the early 1970s, the Common Market of the Six[2] was well established and, just prior to the conclusion of negotiations that led to Britain's accession to the Treaty of Rome, the Luxemburg Treaty had enshrined the financial arrangements for the French-designed Common Agricultural Policy (CAP) into European Law.

Britain would thus have to accept an agricultural arrangement that would cost her dear in the decades to come. In addition Britain's fishing industry was compromised as part of the deal in exchange for membership and it's pretty clear from the records that Britain's space programme met with its demise, as will be shown in the following chapter.

During the first six months of 1972, when the ECA(72) seemed

---

[1] The history of American involvement in the removal of British influence with Europe's future and the European Movement has been examined more fully in the Preface to this book.

[2] Germany, France, Italy, Belgium, Holland and Luxembourg.

certain to pass through Parliament, Jean Monnet, through his Comité d'Action pour les États-Unis d'Europe[3] became involved with Britain's campaign to join the EEC. His role was that of the 'honest broker' facilitating the process of joining and to guide the country towards the next stage of integration.

The tone of ministers' and officials' memos and correspondence indicate that Monnet was held in high regard and there was a willingness to accept the offers of help. At the same time there appears a certain degree of scepticism in some quarters with his involvement, but were keen not to show it. Perhaps they feared that he had the power to sabotage entry, even at that late stage.

Those interested in the history of the period will find the documentation illuminating in as much as it shows the Government telling the nation that they were only negotiating a trading arrangement and there would be *'no loss of essential sovereignty'*[4], when in fact they were discussing the next stages of integration.

There is correspondence on common European action in the monetary field (economic and monetary union), a European monetary fund, anticipating the establishment of a European Investment Bank (EIB), as well as social policy and the EEC's political prospects.

Correspondence shows that the Heath Government was even discussing European external relations anticipating the establishment of a European Union 'Foreign Office', an institution that had to wait another 40 years until the Lisbon Treaty in 2010, brought it to fruition.

Astounding, as it may seem, Monnet even involved himself in the nomination of British European Commissioners, no doubt ensuring

---

[3] Monnet, founded his 'Action Committee' following the rejection of, the European Defence Community (EDC), by the French National Assembly on 30th August, 1954. Monnet, who claimed that EDC was his idea, called this 'a serious crisis for Europe' and resigned from the supranational 'High Authority' that controlled the European Coal and Steel Community (CECA). Monnet writes that after the signing of the Treaty of Rome on 25th March 1957, his 'Action Committee' focused 'on expanding the Community to Great Britain .... '.

[4] Refer to Chapter.1.

they were properly 'on-side'. There is no indication that anyone in Government was concerned with this.

The following letter from Tom Bridges at 10 Downing Street shows the attitude of officials and politicians to Monnet's 'guiding hand':

Writing to Michael Alexander at the FCO, that Heath has suggested: *'that Monnet's idea that the Community* [EEC] *might development an employment policy, "merits further examination"'*.

The mindset of the Government was clearly at odds with its presentation to Parliament and the public.

And Foreign Secretary, Alec Douglas Home, caught up in the euphoria, exhibits an unseemly deference when writing to the man: *'But I would like to say how much I agree with the method which you recommend should be followed in promoting the process of European unification'*.

```
     the Action Committee.

        I have discussed this with Geoffrey Rippon.  I hope
you will forgive me if I do not attempt to comment in detail
on the wide range of proposals contained in your paper.  But
I would like to say how much I agree with the method which
you recommend should be followed in promoting the process
of European unification, at the end of paragraph 2 of the
paper.
        Equally,      agree with the rema
```

This letter by the second most important person in government, shows a strangely contrasting stance with, on the one hand a willingness to covertly confer on European integration with a foreign 'agent' who'd never been elected by anyone and without any mandate to do so, whilst on the other prepared to deceive the British public and Parliament over the Government's true intentions. Will historians writing of this time regard it as one of the blackest periods in the story of the nation?

It's difficult to gauge the motives of Jean Monnet, a man who spent a lifetime involved in international affairs, and it's unclear whether Monnet was self-financing and motivated by some higher purpose, or was acting as an agent of some foreign power.

But there are clues that Monnet was closely involved with the Americans, particularly William ('Bill') Donovan, founder of OSS in WWII.

Donovan was also Chairman of ACUE[5] and working for the CIA until 1955[6]. This date is significant in that it shows that Donovan was still active at the time Monnet founded his 'Action Committee' following the rejection of the EDC in 1954[7]. This raises the possibility that Monnet was induced to alter his campaigning stance following the failure to create a European Army, demonstrating how he was influenced by American interests. The records also show that Monnet maintained his contact with Donovan[8].

That Monnet was honoured for his work with the presentation of the Presidential Medal of Freedom, with Special Distinction, on 6th December 1963 by United States President, Lyndon Johnson, one of only three ever given to non-elected political figures[9], implies services of a most valuable nature to the United States – what could they be?

If Monnet was not acting alone but involved with American clandestine organisations working for a federal Europe, it is perhaps

---

[5] Richard Aldridge in his book 'Hidden Hand', is clear about Monnet's backers, see page. 345: 'Many Americans working for the CIA through ACUE' and other intelligence agencies, 'were central in supporting the three most important 'insider' groups emerging in the 1950s: the European Movement, the Bilderberg Group and Jean Monnet's 'Action Committee for a United States of Europe'.

[6] 'Hidden Hand', by Richard Aldridge, Chapter 16: The CIA's Federalist Operation: ACUE and the European Movement, Page.347.

[7] See footnote 3, Page 26 of this Chapter.

[8] Letter, Monnet to Donovan, 10th March 1952 - American Committee on a United Europe, Georgetown University Manuscripts, Special Collections Centre.

[9] John McCloy, banker, post-war American High Commissioner to Germany, expert on psychological warfare and one of those forming the American branch of the Bildeberg group in 1954, was one of the other two awarded the medal with special distinction . It is also notable that McCloy served on the Warren Commission investigating the assassination of President Kennedy and later served as a consultant to Johnson.

sobering to contemplate an American agent promoting interests contrary to the wishes of the people[10], was overtly stepping through Whitehall corridors of power advising the Prime Minister and senior government ministers and perhaps even influencing decisions. Monnet's intervention seems to have been gratefully received.

---

[10] Refer to chart showing polling results prior to the first reading of ECA(72) – Chapter. 3., Civil service in Action, Broadcast Media Participation.

CHAPTER 5

The mysterious cancellation of Black Arrow
Britain's last satellite launcher rocket[1]

Was Britain's abandonment of its space programme part of the entry price to the EEC?

Black Arrow was a three-stage rocket designed to launch satellites and capable of putting payloads of about 100 kg into low-earth orbit.

It was conceived in 1964 by the Royal Aircraft Establishment (RAE) and was essentially a modification of the 1950s Black Knight sounding rocket[2]. It was expected that after the cancellation of Blue Streak[3] by the Conservative Government in 1960, Black Arrow (pictured right) would keep Britain in space at a modest level of expenditure until costs of a larger rocket capable of launching satellites into synchronous orbit might be justified.

Black Arrow

Black Arrow's relatively small size was indicative of the financial constraints the Wilson Government was operating under, but at least the British space programme was kept alive through the late 1960s. But the small budget of just £9 million left little leeway for trial and error during development. Five Black Arrows were, however, built and four were successfully launched into space at the Woomera test range in Australia, the first in 1968. But it was not surprising, with such

---

[1] This story is largely derived from National Archive records, CAB 164/859.

[2] An instrument-carrying rocket designed to take measurements and perform scientific experiments during its sub-orbital flight. For propulsion a combination of kerosene and high test peroxide was used which was innovative for the time.

[3] Blue Streak was designed as a medium range ballistic missile.

penny-pinching, that one launch failed due to technical problems as did the first attempt at an orbital launch in 1970.

Negotiations

When a Conservative Government replaced Labour in 1970, Black Arrow and the Space Programme became the target of cuts. A Parliamentary Select Committee on the future of the British space effort was due to meet in June 1971, but before the Committee could report, the decision to cancel had been taken precipitously on 24th May 1971, according to a Minute from the Lord Privy Seal's Office dated 27th May 1971.

The official reason given was that the Programme was too costly, which at £1000/day was ridiculous. But the timing of the cancellation, and the fact that negotiations to join the Common Market were in their final delicate stages, raises the suspicion that Britain's Space Programme was sacrificed (there was no other British launcher being considered) to please the French. In fact it is possible that it had been targeted for that reason from the time the Conservative Government took office.

The interests of the fishing industry had already been threatened in negotiations, the Government's negotiators agreeing that all Community vessels would have the same right of access to British waters as British vessels. This could only get worse as more nations joined the Community, as proved to be the case when, periodically, British fishing vessels had to be scrapped to safeguard stocks from over-fishing.

The Common Agricultural Policy (CAP), which in effect meant Britain subsidising French farmers, together with common access to fishing grounds, was a high price in itself to buy into membership of the EEC[4]. That Britain might be required to abandon its Space

---

[4] The CAP was not wholly popular with other members of the 'Six' at the time of Britain's EEC entry negotiations during the first half of 1971. The Italian Prime Minister, Signor Emilo Colombo, at a meeting with the Chancellor of the Duchy of Lancaster, Geoffrey Rippon, Chief negotiator for the British Government, said that the CAP could not go on because of the drain on Community resources and the risk of setting off trade wars. This, he said, was one of the

Programme as well, would need to be hushed up for fear that the total 'give-away' package would be unacceptable to Parliament and the public.

As it was, to the embarrassment of the Heath Government, the last Black Arrow rocket worked perfectly on 28th October 1971 (after cancellation had already been decided and made public), launching 'Prospero', Britain's first (experimental) satellite into orbit. It was placed into a 50,000 km orbit and it continues to circle the Earth every 100 minutes. Rocket engineers, scientists and support staff were then sacked.

With the correct equipment[5], it is understood, the satellite's radio transmitter can be 'heard' transmitting on 137.56 MHz.

So what was the sequence of events that led to the untimely demise of Britain's short-lived Space Programme?

Notable Successes

The records show that it was the Wilson Government who had initiated the Black Arrow Rocket Programme in November 1966, albeit under very tight financial constraints. When Heath came to power with a small majority on the 18th June 1970, Black Arrow was well into its programme of development and, as we have seen, had carried out tests flights on the Woomera rocket range in Australia.

However, less than a month after the election, it looked like the new Conservative Government were less than enthusiastic about 'Space'. The first indication of this is a plea from an anxious Colonel R.W. Millo of the Ministry of Technology who seems to have got wind of

---

reasons for Italian support for British entry.

Rippon's negative response to this invitation to help deal with CAP, was that 'we' had not asked for change to the Common Agricultural Policy because 'we' realised that, in Mr Harold Wilson's words, it was not negotiable – extracted from minutes of meeting with Italian negotiators, March 29th - April 27th, 1971; National Archive records, CAB 164/859.

[5] BBC Coast's Alice Roberts presented a programme from the Isle of Wight's High Down rocket static test site by the Needles in 2011. Black Arrow rockets had been tested at High Down prior to shipment to Woomera for launching. During the programme a receiver was set up and it was claimed the signal received was from the Prospero satellite still orbiting the Earth.

a threat to Black Arrow.

In a letter addressed to R.A. Neate, Head of the Space Administration Branch, dated 15th July 1970, Col. Millo wrote that: ' *... the relatively little cost of the space technology programme, has already enabled the UK to attain some notable successes in international contracts and helped to sustain our credibility as a forward looking technological nation*'. His letter records the small amount spent in comparison with France, Germany and Japan.

Several hand-written notes in the file, essentially show that Col. Millo's promotion of Black Arrow was unwanted and kicked 'into the long grass', the appeal 'falling on deaf ears' and ignored.

Then Maurice Macmillan MP, son of Harold Macmillan, Prime Minister until his resignation in 1964, in response to the new Government's spending review, is recommending cost cutting in technology. In a memorandum to John Davies, Minister of Technology, dated 3rd August 1970, Macmillan writes: '*we should take as our aim a 50% saving in the Technological Support Programme.* Macmillan, although generally supportive of space projects, reveals that Black Arrow was under review, thus justifying Col. Millo's fears.

This would seem to show that the new regime might have an antipathy towards matters technological. In his memorandum, Macmillan added unhelpfully that it was the business of private industry to finance high-tech ventures[6].

However, it was not just cost, if that was ever really a factor. The following pages make the case that Black Arrow was in fact cancelled in a deal with the French that persuaded them to remove their veto over British membership of the EEC.

Crucial talks had been arranged for Heath to meet French President Pompidou in Paris in an attempt to 'ease tensions' between the two countries. The historic meeting took place on Thursday and Friday,

---

[6] At the time of writing, Richard Branson's private venture space vehicle: Virgin Galactic has recently broken up and crashed in the Mojave desert in the USA. It was the second private venture space vehicle to meet a similar fate in the course of a few days raising doubts over the feasibility of such non-governmental missions.

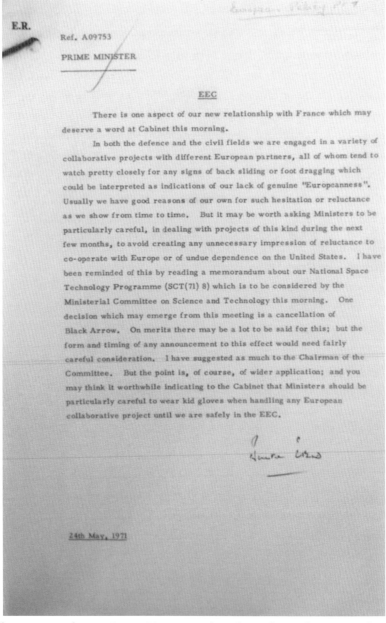

The memorandum to Prime Minister, Edward Heath, on the proposed cancellation of Black Arrow – Monday morning following the conclusion of 'successful talks' in Paris with President Pompidou (Friday, 21st May).

the 20th and 21st May 1971 and saw an instant warming in relations, with Heath declaring on his return that Friday evening to London, "the talks were a great success".

If the sudden and unexpected thaw in relations resulted from some sort of deal, on top of CAP and fisheries already conceded, then that would very likely have had severe public repercussions if it ever got out – it didn't, not then anyway.

The first thing the following Monday morning, a memorandum headed just 'EEC' (see facing page) was addressed to the Prime Minister, signed (signatory unclear), by an unidentified person[7]. The memorandum referred to the scheduled morning meeting of the 'Ministerial Committee on Science and Technology (MCST)'[8], with Black Arrow cancellation the main item on the agenda.

The memo betrays a sense of urgency and apprehension and is particularly ambiguous, as though there was a fear the deal could come unglued, yet what had been agreed 'dared not speak its name' – the memo rings of what is known in the trade as, *'studied ambiguity'*. The underlying message expressed seems to be that cabinet ministers attending the late morning meeting should do the right thing, without perhaps some, or any, of them being sure why they were expected to cancel Black Arrow that day.

The memo is in effect advice to the Prime Minister on how he should tell cabinet ministers to behave at the morning's meeting, without him actually giving them the reason. But it is hard to credit that any of those present would not have grasped that the meeting, and what cabinet ministers were being called upon to do, was unconnected with the Paris talks and Heath's triumphant return to London the previous Friday.

For: be 'sufficiently European (*Europeanness*)', not '*backsliding*', not

---

[7] Memorandum possibly signed by or for Douglas Hurd, Heath's Political Secretary at No.10 and one of Heath's small delegation to Paris.

[8] The subject matter of the meeting was spelled out in a memo dated 20th May (first day of talks in Paris) to the MCST providing guidance as to the decision to be made – cancellation of Black Arrow.

'foot dragging', or a *'reluctance to co-operate with Europe'* looks very much like diplomatic code for 'scrap Black Arrow'; for: *'the Cabinet and Ministers should be particularly careful to wear kid gloves when handling any European collaborative project until we are safely in the EEC[9]*, reads: 'don't let Parliament or the public know of the cancellation before we have got into the Common Market'. The concern is not with the public or Parliament per se, but only that they might make such a fuss that it causes the EEC application to fail – for the 3rd time.

The memo main points are:

1. *'In both defence and civil fields we are engaged in a variety of collaborative projects with different European partners, all of whom tend to watch pretty closely for signs of back sliding or foot dragging which could be interpreted as indications of our lack of genuine "Europeanness".'*

It then turns to the main subject of the meeting, Black Arrow:

2. *'.... but the form and timing of any announcement to this effect* [cancellation of Black Arrow] *would need fairly careful consideration.'*

That 'Space' was expected to be on the Agenda (see Page.39) for the Paris talks and that Pompidou removed his personal veto on Britain's membership the preceding Friday, something major must have taken place – but records of the talks show just talk, not agreements made.

The tone of the memo to the PM is notable in that there's a hint of a lack of deference, although of course there may be a tradition of political secretaries writing in that way. And there is a hint of anxiety that the Prime Minister might back track on any 'agreement' in Paris, for fear of the political consequences should the cancellation leak out, but then it was Heath who would have to 'carry the can' if things went wrong. It was altogether a strange memo.

The Black Arrow file is extensive, yet there are no minutes of the meeting of 24th May of the Ministerial Committee on Science and Technology. We know that minutes were taken, since the minutes,

---

[9] The author of the memo makes the EEC sound like some sort of lifeboat.

were referred to (see to below) in the memorandum from the Private Secretary to the Lord Privy Seal, confirming the Prime Minister had read them and caused him to issue his instructions on how to handle the public relations issues over the cancellation.

Without the minutes, we cannot know what actually took place, we do not even know whether the meeting was made privy to the 'real' reason for the cancellation and if so what was said. We don't know why the Minutes are not in the file. Were they weeded before deposition at the National archives, or never included? Whichever, it shows the Government were in quite a stir over the issue.

This author wrote a letter to the Heath's political secretary, Douglas Hurd on 2nd August 2006 asking him if he knew anything about the cancellation. The reply dated, 9th August, stated that he, Hurd, did not attend cabinet meetings and was not involved in policy discussions such as the ones in question and could not throw any light on the problem being researched.

The cancellation generated as much paper over two months as there had been over the previous six years of the project and is mostly concerned with what to tell the French and public, and when. The file ends abruptly on 3rd August 1971 after the cancellation had been announced in the House of Commons at the end of July in a written question and written answer.

Belated 'French Interest' (post cancellation)

The story of Black Arrow did not end quite there with the 24th May cancellation meeting. Bizarrely, just four days after the Paris talks, a dispatch dated Tuesday, 25th May, is received from the French proposing a collaborative effort in Space employing Britain's Black Arrow rocket.

The Government, more particularly Heath himself, needed to conceal cancellation of Black Arrow from the French for a few weeks until negotiations in Brussels on the EEC had been completed[10] and

---

[10] Not the real reason, but Heath needed stalling time so that he could consider how best to present the bad news without too much notice being taken – there appears to have been no debate on the subject in Parliament, Black Arrow just faded from the scene. From that time on Britain lost any hopes of having an independently controlled nuclear deterrent, being entirely reliant upon

they were 'safely in'. A memorandum (27th May) from B.T. Gilmore, Private Secretary to the Lord Privy Seal, three days after the Ministerial Committee meeting, refers to the Prime Minister's requests regarding Black Arrow:

'*The Prime Minister has seen the minutes of the meeting of the Ministerial Committee on Science and Technology* [Heath is not listed as a participant] *which the Lord Privy Seal* [Earl Jellicoe] *chaired on 24th May ....* . *He noted that it was proposed, following the replacement* [there was no replacement, but use of the word 'cancellation' was clearly too sensitive] *of Black Arrow, that we should rely on the American 'Scout Launcher' and that this should be explained to the French, who have a launcher of their own (the Diamant), before the* [general] *announcement.*

The Prime Minister has asked that no further action [regarding cancellation] *should be taken on this, and in particular no approach made to the French until he has had an opportunity to look into this further with the Lord Privy Seal. ....11* '

Blue Streak, cancelled by the Conservative Government in 1960
Deutsches Museum Flugwerft Schleissheim

Taken at face value, this letter makes no sense if the French were party to the Black Arrow cancellation deal, it only makes sense with that knowledge. And without that knowledge the French collaborative proposal for Black Arrow would have seemed genuine enough.

America for a delivery system.
11 Appears like stalling for time.

SECRET

TOPICS TO RAISE WITH PRESIDENT POMPIDOU

A.   (i)   Community Finance

      (ii) New Zealand butter and cheese

      (iii) Sugar from the developing
            Commonwealth countries

      (iv) Agricultural transition
            including Community preference.

B.   Sterling (sterling balances and reserve role)
      and Capital Movements.

C.   Future of Europe (including relations with
      the United States and the Commonwealth)

      (i)   Political and Institutions

      (ii) Defence

      (iii) Economic, Commercial and Monetary.

D.   East West relations.

E.   French language and "cultural package".

F.   Relations between Anglophone and Francophone Africa.

TOPICS PRESIDENT POMPIDOU MAY RAISE:
DEFENSIVE BRIEFS REQUIRED.

G.   The neutrals (EFTA non-candidates).

H.   Technology:

      (i)   Concorde

      (ii) Channel Tunnel

      (iii) Centrifuge

      (iv) Space

I.   Site of Community Institutions (unlikely to be
      raised.

SECRET

Agenda for talks between PM Heath and President Pompidou in Paris
20th, 21st, May 1971 in Paris – note: 'Space' is the final Agenda item.

As stated above, the offer came through a letter written just 4 days after the Paris talks, dated Tuesday 25th May 1971, from General Aubiniere, Directeur General of the Centre National Détudes Spatiales, to Mr Goodson[12]. Aubiniere was calling for a joint programme employing their own 'Diamant' launcher in combination with 'Black Arrow'. Of course the timing of the proposed venture makes sense in the context of a coordinated public deception plan.

Whether General Aubiniere was required to write to Mr Goodson at the Cabinet Office knowing it to be a deception plan matters little, he did it.

There is much on file making perhaps too much of the PM's wish to keep cancellation from the French. The emphasis on concealment tends only to confirm the interpretation of events described here.

During this time of elation, mixed with panic, confusion and even perhaps fear, Heath may have been pondering the historical record – did Heath, knowing the records would have to be made public eventually, want the truth hidden in perpetuity? If it was a good deal for Heath, it was not a deal good for Heath's legacy, if the truth got out.

By July, negotiations in Brussels with the 'Six' on terms of EEC entry were successfully concluded. This was the cue for the Prime Minister to declare at a 7th July 1971 meeting, that concealment of the cancellation of Black Arrow from the French was no longer necessary:

'Now that Common Market negotiations are over; and relations with the French are more friendly, there is no reason to conceal what we are really thinking ...... [cancellation of Black Arrow]'.

This is revealing. At the same meeting as Heath announced that concealment is no longer necessary, he proclaimed the French have called off their proposed rocket collaboration with Britain: ' ...... *nor have the French any further use for Black Arrow'*. It looks so phoney that it can only have been a staged event with the three events related

---

12 Of the Cabinet Office.

dragoon Britain into the so called Common Market. The subject of this section is the part played in this by the European Movement.

The European Movement (EM), was of immense value to Heath in that it gave the appearance of being unconnected with government. It presented an image of itself as drawing support from ordinary members of the public, i.e. a sort of grass roots organisation. This image was far removed from reality.

However, the records make clear that the European Movement was an integral part of a highly effective governmental propaganda machine, collaborating (or rather colluding) to 'shoe-horn' the British people into the EEC – whether they liked it or not. There was close coordination between Government departments and the EM (as well as the British Council and the Conservative Group for Europe (CGE)).

European Movement funding in Britain from the CIA seems to have dried up at the time of Heath's application to join the EEC, but it was now receiving regular funding from the Government by way of FCO annual grants. More surprising than that, was that the EM was co-opted onto the Government's planning team, and worked as an almost equal, but vital partner – these days they would be called 'stake-holders' to bestow a semblance of respectability.

The EM was proactive throughout the country and provided speakers for public and party political meetings and the FCO's Information Research Department (IRD) was mobilised to provide '*advice and help*' to them. The EM reported at one meeting (at the height of the campaign) in the Lord President's (William Whitelaw's) office that they were providing 600 speakers a month. And at the same meeting, documents reveal: Norman Reddaway head of IRD was worried that, although they had the capacity to produce letters for the campaign, it did not have the machinery to distribute them. The EM undertook this work and received substantial Government funding to do so, thus undermining any claim to be a grass roots organisation.

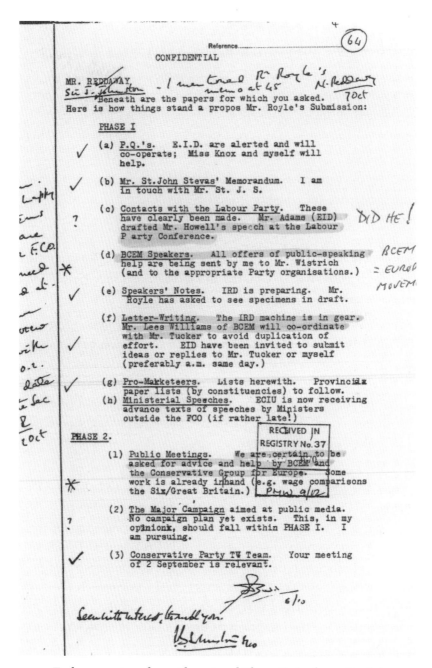

Early campaign plans, Phase I and Phase II, Anthony Royle's plan submitted to Norman Reddaway – 1970

IRD wrote letters for the EM to place in the press and the European Information Department (EID) was mobilised to '*provide ideas for reply*' to the EM the same morning as letters from '*antis*' appeared

... a number of other organisations. The EEC's London Information Office worked closely with the European Movement in promoting visits from this country to Brussels. Visitors were used as speakers and sometimes appeared on television in addition to their regular programmes of informal meetings.

... books related to British membership of the Community. A simple "question and answer" booklet produced by the Movement was written by IRD as were two other booklets. The Movement also produced a lively and popular journal The British European which was

distributed ... million ... lets of ... and 3 million copies of The British European during the campaign. IRD also wrote pamphlets for publication by the Conservative Group for Europe and the Conservative Research Centre.

in the press. The EM would then use EID's replies for members to

awkwardly used from the campaign's point of view.
7.   Furthermore it did seem likely that Mr. Goodhart would pursue the idea of a referendum in his constituency. If so, the BCEM would in any case attempt to discredit it in advance; if it did take place, they would fight it vigorously.
8.   On the general trend in the country Mr. Freeman said that th...

sign before sending to the particular newspaper. Opposition campaigners were thus prevented from ever building up a case due to the army of Civil Servants briefing against them.

In spite of the advantage of a one-sided campaign, the Government were fearful they could be forced to concede a referendum on the country joining the Common Market, a referendum which they expected to lose – so they were determined there wouldn't be one. The EM were charged by the Government to campaign against one

out that the EEC Information Unit produced extremely good material but felt as a foreign organisation that it could not distribute it too widely. It was agreed that the BCEM should distribute the Unit's material on a wide scale under its own auspices. Sir Tufton Beamish said he thought effective distribution was beyond the powers of the BCEM and that a full-time professional should be employed. Mr. Freeman said that the BCEM would in fact employ direct mail organisations to undertake the distribution. Mr. Reddaway said that it was extremely important

and worked to '*discredit it in advance*'[4].

The EM also colluded with Brussels. The London-based EEC Information Unit, as a foreign organisation, could not directly involve itself in the campaign, so the EM stepped in again, providing an indirect means for their participation by '*distributing their material*' on a wide-scale using '*direct mail organisations to undertake the distribution*'.

---

[4] Activities to resist a referendum are discussed in Chapter.10.

That the EM worked hand in hand with the Heath Government as if part of its machinery, is recorded again in the post-Campaign report of 15th February 1972. It was compiled by Anthony Royle, MP – a Foreign Office minister.

```
on the handling of the media.  IRD as one ...
set up a special editorial/research section to work
closely with the ECIU.  The IRD/ECIU co-operation
produced the basic material on which most of the
subsequent productions were based - booklets,
talking points, speeches, notes, etc.  Thus
throughout the winter of 1970-71 all the infrastructure
was laid down, the preparatory work initiated and
the ground prepared by the European Movement in
consultation with FCO Departments.  The European
Movement used this time to strengthen its own
regional
```

Royle wrote: '*The IRD/ECIU co-operation produced the basic material on which most of the subsequent productions were based – booklets, talking points, speeches, notes etc. Thus throughout the winter of 1970-71 all the infrastructure was laid down, the preparatory work initiated and the ground prepared for the European Movement in consultation with the FCO departments..... . This preparatory work ensured that the Government's open[5] campaign* [Royle means public campaign] *was launched and carried out so effectively between July and October 1971'*.

Royle's Report highlighted the extra funding [tax money] gifted by the FCO during the campaign: '*The FCO's annual grant of £7,500 to the European Movement for its own visits programme was topped up several times, and smaller donations were made to other organisations'*.

The report noted: '*The EEC's London Information Office worked closely with the European Movement in promoting visits from this country to Brussels'*. These Brussels' junkets for 'soft' targets, continue to this day.

---

[5] Note the use of the word 'open', this book has discovers many aspects of the 'close' campaign, but of course that does not mean that everything has been revealed.

The EM, presumably using Government or corporate money, appointed a firm of advertising consultants '*to organise an advertising*

> advertising campaign, and a survey of public
> attitudes was commissioned. Corporate members
> of the Movement were asked to assist by including
> an EEC element in their own advertisements: The
> Times and British Leyland, in particular, produced
> a number of advertisements with an EEC content.
>
> 13.   The Movement's advertising campaign reached
> its climax in the period July-October 1971, but a
> number of advertisements were placed in the national

campaign, and [a] *survey of public attitudes was commissioned. Corporate members of the Movement were asked to assist by including an EEC element in their own advertising*'. The Times and British Leyland (see excerpt

> LETTERS TO THE PRESS AND PUBLIC
>
> 15.   Between September 1970 and October 1971 IRD
> kept up a steady stream of letters and articles
> to the Press, working closely with the European
> Movement, and also drafted the replies to over
> 2,000 letters from the general public.

from Royle's Report above) duly complied. The Movement's advertising campaign reached a climax in the period July 1970 – October 1971 (timed for the crucial First Reading of the Bill, ECA(72), in Parliament).

The report continued: '*Between September 1970* [3 months after Heath's election victory] *and October 1971, IRD kept up a steady stream of letters and articles to the press, working closely with the European Movement, …*'

Today it is clear that the European Movement was an indispensable and integral part of the Government's campaign, but those campaigning against EEC membership were completely unaware of this, having no idea of the corporatist

also, of course, did many ...

66. Of the other elements of the campaign, BCEM advertising in the national and local press, including articles and lists of prominent supporters, was generally agreed to have been very effective. Their poster and sticker advertising was perhaps less so. Their conferences, seminars, rallies, mobile vans, anti-referenda and other activities all made their
/contribution,

- 40 -

SECRET

forces ranged against them. The Government was never able to persuade more than 51% of the public, and only for a short few critical months at that, of the merits of joining the EEC. This was in spite of the participation of the EM and that the EEC was presented as harmless, being just a trading arrangement.

to reach their aims."

4 /0 rr

60. The campaign cost the Government £461,400 and the BCEM under £250,000, a total of about £711,400. The Government expenditure was on the production and advertising of the Popular Version of the White Paper (4 million copies of which were distributed) and the Factsheets (16½ million together with 3½ million of two compendia). There was some running criticism of this expenditure from the anti-Marketeers in Parliament in July. Ministers were able to defend it, success...

Without this help and deception, the Government could never have won the narrow vote (to enter) in Parliament at the Second Reading – the majority being reduced to just eight (no whole-hearted consent) when the facts had been digested.

Anthony Royle in his Report concludes: '*BCEM* [EM] *advertising in the national and local press, including articles and list of prominent supporters, was generally agreed to have been very effective ...... anti-referenda and other activities all made their contribution, particularly at grass roots level. The campaign for letters to MPs was limited. The other arrangements for letters* [written by IRD] *to the press on the other hand worked splendidly*'.

The funding of the Campaign, Royle reported, cost the Government £461,400 and the European Movement under £250,000. These were huge sums for the time, and ignored the costs of civil servants employed on the campaign and the effect of their diversion from their normal task of the running the nation.

The EM acted effectively as a quasi-governmental department, posing to the public as a grass roots campaigning movement. They were in fact working to undermine sovereignty and hard-won freedoms, justice and democracy. But of course the Heath Government mobilised to its cause any organisation or individual it could persuade to help, in this instance, to publish or re-publish pamphlets), these 'helpers' included:

The Conservative Research Department and Political
Centre (were Conservative donors and members informed
of this?)

Chatham House[6]

PEP[7]

---

[6] Chatham House, also know as the Royal Institute of International Affairs (RIIA). Chatham House was the residence of three Prime Ministers: Pitt the Elder, Edward Stanley and William Gladstone. RIIA was instituted soon after WWI together with sister organisation, The Council on Foreign relations (CFR) in the USA, with a view to preventing future wars! Chatham House received the Royal Charter in 1926.

[7] The author could not determine the identity of PEP.

The NFU

The Economist

Barclays Bank

> .... published or republished by the Conservative
> Research Department and Political Centre, Chatham House,
> PEP, the NFU, the Economist, Barclays, Lloyds and
> Westminster Banks and the European Communities'
> Information Office in London as well as by the BCEM
> and its various associated organisations – a total of
> over 50 pamphlets in all, with authors including
> Ministers. MPs, researchers and journalists.' The

Lloyds Bank

Wesminster Bank

This meant global bankers were buying into government, undermining the principle of: 'government of the people, by the people, for the people'.

CHAPTER 7

Participation by Brussels

That the EEC had the status of a foreign power before Britain joined and therefore, by convention, should not interfere in the affairs of another sovereign country, did not seem to bother the organisation, its officials, nor for that matter, did it bother the Heath Government.

We have seen earlier the interfering from Jean Monnet (and his Comité d'Action pour les États-Unis d'Europe) and the willing collaboration of the Government through the FCO's European Integration Department (IRD), but it's not widely known that the Brussels' machinery was involved, clandestinely, in the campaign against the British public.

Anthony Royle reported in: 'Approach to Europe', that: '*The EEC's London Information Office worked closely with the European Movement in promoting visits from this country to Brussels*'. These all expenses paid trips were gifted to those who were seen as susceptible to that sort of thing and who might help promote a pro-EEC line – beware of '*Greeks bearing gifts*'.

The European Communities Office in London was also prepared to help, and did so by providing pamphlets for the public information campaign. The Heath Government did not complain as far as the records show.

The EEC Information Unit's activities in the UK also figure in the record of the meeting of 31st March 1971. This was held in the Lord President's (William Whitelaw's) office. The aforementioned

> out that the EEC Information Unit produced extremely good material but felt as a foreign organisation that it could not distribute it too widely. It was agreed that the BCEM should distribute the Unit's material on a wide scale under its own auspices. Sir Tufton Beamish said he thought effective distribution was beyond the powers of the BCEM and that a full-time professional should be employed. Mr. Freeman said that the BCEM would in fact employ direct mail organisations to undertake the distribution.
>
> Mr. Raddaway said

Mr Adams, pointed out that, '*the EEC Information Unit produced extremely good material but felt as a foreign organisation that it could not distribute it too widely*'. The Government's willing, and always available, European Movement, normally present at top Government meetings, stepped in: '*It was agreed that the BCEM should distribute the Unit's material on a wide scale under its own auspices*'.

CHAPTER 8

Town Twinning

Before Edward Heath took Britain into the Common Market there pre-existed a few bona-fide Town Twinning Associations operating exchange visits between British and continental towns and cities – the first associations coming into being after the Second World War.

The Government, however, viewed them as a potential 'Trojan Horse' to be employed to consolidate the success gained in Parliament with the Third Reading of the ECA(72) in July 1972. Some continental European Movement branches were already making them part of the propaganda operation, particularly in France.

Although there was briefly 'level pegging' in opinion polls at the height of the Information Campaign in 1972, the effect was short-lived. It was clear the campaign had not changed public opinion on a permanent basis and something had to be done.

Anthony Royle, the FCO minister and author, as we have seen above, of the paper 'An Approach to Europe', was tasked with rectifying the situation and set about visiting French Mayors[1] from 27th October 1972. Although the Campaign had already been won and the European Communities Bill 1972 passed, the Government was concerned with keeping the public on side and preparing the ground for further integration (although the public were told nothing of this).

> 1. I submit a Speaking Note for Mr Royle's use at his meeting with French Mayors on 27 October.
>
> 2. We would like to interest the French Mayors in town-twinning with British towns and the note therefore concentrates on this element in the £6 million programme. If any of the
> .... follow this up, Mr Royle could suggest

---

[1] French Mayors usually oversee town twinning (Jumelage) and is part of Movement Européean in France.

In a memo on town twinning from the FCO's European Integration Department (EID) to Norman Reddaway and others, the writer (J M Crosby) discloses the Government's budget for this activity:

'......*and the note therefore concentrates on this element of the £6 million programme'*.

This was a huge amount in 1972.

So Town Twinning lost its innocence and was drawn into the plot being used to soften up members for further steps in the integration process. There was an exchange of 'officers' between the European Movement and Town Twinning Associations in the UK and it is not unusual for EM members to be seen chairing town twinning association annual general meetings. So the two, at least administratively, are closely related.

It would be unfair to suggest though, that those participating in town twinning exchanges are motivated by a desire for European integration[2]. For the most part they simply want to enjoy the interchange with different peoples and cultures. After all, it is the differences between peoples which make it worthwhile to associate in the first place. But there often seems to be an undercurrent of EU promotional activity and it does not go unnoticed that the French Twinning Association is a part of the Mouvement Européen which sometimes puts on EU promotional themes in their Mairies (town halls).

The European Union ingratiated itself into Town Twinning movements in 1989 by providing financial support for twinning visits, provided there were no 'folkloristic' events involved in the visit. Towns wishing to twin with continental towns were then required to have their mayor swear an oath of allegiance to the EU.

The Town Twinning movement website showed its close links: '*To meet the objectives of bringing citizens closer together the European Commission, has since 1989, been running an annual programme to support town twinning schemes which it regards as a valuable way of involving ordinary people and their elected representatives in European integration*

---

[2] This writer has personal knowledge of members who do not support Britain's membership of the EU.

and of strengthening their sense of belonging to the European Union', i.e. the money came with strings.

Another passage reads: '*A programme for the meeting which is not merely touristic: folkloristic events* [a distraction] *and commercial exchanges are not co-financed. From 1999 onwards, support will only be granted if a special theme (i.e. European citizenship, European Union and its impact on local authorities, topical European policy issues such as, for example, the Amsterdam Treaty, the single currency, European elections, enlargement, and other ongoing policy areas, e.g. employment, a social Europe, culture, Common Agricultural Policy, etc) is included in the meeting programme'*.

The oath of allegiance reads: '*We take a solemn oath:*

To maintain permanent ties between our municipalities....... .'

and: '*To join forces so as to further, to the best of our ability, the success of this vital enterprise of peace and prosperity: THE EUROPEAN UNION'*.

The Town Twinning movement was hooked, lined and sinkered.

CHAPTER 9

Convincing Conservative rank and file

Following its June 1970 election victory, the Conservative Party leadership moved swiftly to gain the support of Party rank and file membership for joining the European Economic Community. Geoffrey Rippon, Chancellor of the Duchy of Lancaster, was appointed leader of the delegation sent to Brussels to negotiate Britain's terms of entry. At the Conservative Party conference that October, he spoke at length to convince members of the merits of Britain joining.

Geoffrey Rippon

One has to ask what happened to the assurance given at the conference to the Party faithful, that: *'We shall not sign a Treaty of Accession which would commit us to the common fisheries policy, or to any agreement which did not satisfactorily protect our legitimate interests'*. Comforting words maybe, but as time was to show, it was the language of deceit designed to achieve goals not shared by the greater part of the electorate.

> We shall not sign a Treaty of Accession which would commit us to the present common fisheries policy, or to any arrangement which did not satisfactorily protect our legitimate interests.
>
> The essential ob̶j̶e̶c̶t̶i̶v̶e̶

Later in his speech, Rippon also provided reassurance on sovereignty: *'So it is nonsense to say that Britain will no longer be ruled*

> So it is nonsense to say
> that Britain will no longer be
> ruled by the will of the people's
> representatives – or to put it in
> constitutional terms – by the
> Queen in Parliament.

by the rule of the people's representatives – or to put it in constitutional terms – by the Queen in Parliament'. Compare this with the FCO 30/1048 report drawn up in the following months which provided a different and gloomy view of the prospects for Britain's sovereignty after entry. This was a view realised by subsequent events and especially the headlong rush to a European Union Constitution (Lisbon Treaty)[1], intended to overshadow or replace the Bill of Rights, Magna Carta and other constitutional documents.

It's not surprising that the game played by politicians and officials at the time, required that FCO 30/1048 be hidden from the public by official secrecy until the year 2000. No doubt the conspirators concluded that by the year 2000, the events of 1970-72, would no longer be of particular public interest – they were wrong, and no new Cameron Bill of Rights will rectify the illegitimacy of EU membership.

---

[1] The EU's initial attempt to impose a constitution failed when both France and the Netherlands rejected it in referenda. These democratic results were snubbed by Brussels when replaced by another Constitutional document, similar to the one before. This one, wrapped up with the word 'constitution' removed, and re-named 'The Lisbon Treaty'. This one was rejected as well, this time by Ireland, but the electorate were forced to vote again when it was approved.

CHAPTER 10

Resisting a Referendum on joining

The one thing Edward Heath, his backers and accomplices feared in their crusade to join the EEC, was a referendum. The documentation reveals a concerted effort by the Government and its agent, the European Movement, to head off demands for one.

Geoffrey Rippon leading the debate for the Government in the House of Commons, made sure it didn't happen. Fending off a question on the subject from Tony Benn, Rippon in the Third and final Reading of the Bill[1], claimed that the Government was authorised to present the legislation[2] to the House, and then contemptuously dismissed Benn with: '*I say in relation to the Right hon. Gentleman's third intervention that he is more characteristic of a cockerel who believes that the sun gets up in the morning simply to hear him crow*'[3]. That was it, a referendum never happened.

Labour MP, Douglas Jay, complained that the three other applicant (to join the EEC) countries were all conducting referenda, one of whom, Norway, rejected membership. Norway has prospered outside ever since.

It was true however, referenda were an innovation in the UK at the time. But Heath, although he had proposed one for Northern Ireland and that joining the EEC was an issue involving fundamental change to the Constitution and the way the country was to be governed, never addressed the matter as far as is known.

Tony Benn was the leading proponent campaigning for one and no doubt irritated the Government front bench with his 'embarrassing' challenges. The establishment, were not going to entertain the idea and briefed against those proposing one. Anthony Royle's report[4]

---

[1] Hansard, 13th July 1971, Column.1867
[2] Alluding perhaps to the constitutional issues involved.
[3] Debate on European Communities Bill, 3rd Reading, 13th July 1972, Hansard, Column. 867.
[4] Approach to Europe, 1970/71, National Archive document, FCO 26/1215.

of events, described those seeking a referendum as '*anti-Parliamentary*[5]': '*The anti-Parliamentary tendency found expression in a*

> into the Communities in the end. The anti-Parliamentary
> tendency found expression in a movement fanned by
> Mr. Wedgwood Benn, for a national referendum on the
> issue; although, in the face of firm Government (and
> official Opposition) rejection, this movement never

movement fanned by Mr Wedgewood Benn for a national referendum on the issue ...... it demanded attention through much of the campaign and in Parliament'.

That there was no serious demand for a referendum on joining from the public was probably due to ignorance of the huge constitutional implications involved – and the authorities had no intention of enlightening them. Additionally, because the waters were muddied by repetition of the mantra: that there was 'no essential loss of sovereignty' involved, and the fact that referenda were untried (being described by the Government at least, as 'un-British'), helps to explain why those advocating one, failed. In any case the public had few ways of making their feelings known and no supporting organisation with which to coalesce around[6] – the government held all the trump cards.

The impact of the European Movement's efforts in talking down a referendum can only be guessed at, but the fact that they did so, showed their determination to exclude the public from having any serious influence on the question of who was to rule them in the future. This should have been a matter of vital importance to everyone, since the issue concerned who would be governing them in the future, but it wasn't.

In retrospect, it is clear that Heath's pledge of not joining without

---

[5] Language to denigrate those opposing the Government's 'European' policies, was carefully employed to discredit them in the eyes of the public. '*Anti-Parliamentary*', was a term that implied that parliament was supreme, and opposition orchestrated outside of Parliament was therefore anti-democratic.

[6] There is no evidence of any polling on the matter, the media were not interested in giving the issue publicity.

the '*full-hearted consent of Parliament and the people*', was broken, and the fact that a referendum was refused was profoundly anti-democratic. The legitimacy of membership, as a result, is challenged to this day, which is unsurprising.

The subsequent, cynical attempt, by Harold Wilson's Government to retrospectively legitimise membership through the 1975 referendum would not repair the damage. Legislation passed by illicit means cannot be legitimised retrospectively by later holding a referendum[7].

They wanted a referendum in 1972, but didn't get one

We can see an echo of this in more recent times with John Prescott's October 2004 retrospective referendum held to legitimise the

---

[7] Ex post facto legislation to legitimise something that was previously illegal, is banned by the constitution in most states.

already appointed and illegitimate, North East England Regional Assembly (NEERA). NEERA was set up in 1999. It was one of eight English regions, part of the EU's Europe-wide regionalisation programme, to 'divide and rule'[8].

The public, more aware than they were in 1971, decisively rejected the setting up of an elected North East Regional Assembly, by more than three to one. in the vote held on 4th November, 2004.

---

[8] Of the eight English appointed regional assemblies (London had a different arrangement), only one, NEERA, was given a referendum. Referenda were to be held later in the remaining seven English regions, following that in the North East. But Prescott abandoned elected regional assemblies altogether because the result in the North East was so unfavourable. That left English Regional Assemblies unelected. The present position and the powers held by regional assemblies is unclear.

CHAPTER 11

The Parliamentary 'Stitch-up'

In the early months of 1971, polls showed public opinion consistently running at more than 3 to 1 against joining the EEC. However, just a few months later, in July, support and opposition were evenly balanced. The graph below shows that it wasn't until June that opinion had begun to shift to any extent, but by the Autumn views were already returning to what they had been at the beginning of the year.

What had brought about this amazing mid-year turnaround? Well, as we have seen in preceding chapters, the Government had set in motion a one-sided, expensive publicity campaign to brainwash the

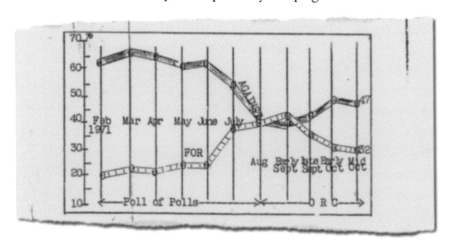

Poll of polls, February to Mid-October 1971

public into accepting they had been wrong. According to the Heath Government, a Government that may have had access to Labour campaign strategy at the election in 1970, Britain just had to join the then, Common Market, an organisation that was not what it was purported to be. It is unsurprising that the movement in the polls coincided with the intensity of the publicity campaign. Polls didn't really reflect the reasoned opinion of the public, but only demonstrated the short term power of advertising.

It also showed that Heath's promise that he would only go in (join the EEC) with the *'full hearted consent of Parliament and the people'* was an empty promise – now common practise in the 21st century. But instead he had taken Britain in using the might of the Government's and Government supported European Movement's publicity machines instead. That meant EEC membership had no basis for support and besides being unconstitutional, was also lacking in moral legitimacy and continues to do so today.

The objective of the massive publicity campaign in July 1971 had been to convince MPs that the tide of public opinion was moving in favour of joining the Common Market giving them cause to vote positively and overwhelmingly for the First Reading of the European Communities Bill (ECA72) that October. The campaign achieved that of course, but at the Second Reading the following February when MPs had a better understanding of what was at stake, the Bill came close to failure. Had only 4 votes been cast the other way it would have done so. There was no *'whole-hearted consent'* promised by Edward Heath at the 1970 General election – but that did not put a stop to it.

The following account provides readers with insight into the Parliamentary 'stitch-up' that helped to set the country on course for division and recrimination that has continued unabated to this day.

Conservative Whips' Report – free or whipped vote?

It's not unusual for governments to use whips to persuade their MPs to adhere to the party line to get legislation through Parliament. The report by Norman St John Stevas, later elevated to Lord St John of Fawsley for his determined work on Europe, examined the merits of a whipped vote against a non-whipped vote. Stevas pondered the question: *'Clearly the question whether to have a whipped vote or a free vote on our side is a vital and complicated one'*. The decision, until Heath

won a decisive majority in favour of entry at the 1st Reading, implying that the 2nd and 3rd readings were undermined by this and unimportant – nothing could be further from the reality of the situation.

But Shore was having none of this, responding (Col. 294)[8] that: '*The vote of 28th October had been taken long before negotiations were over, long before the 43 volumes*[9] *were published and the other 10 volumes*[10] *were published here last week, long before we saw the Treaties of Accession. The right hon. and learned Gentleman will have to think up something better than that*'.

This exchange is important since, in effect, Rippon and through him the Government, was claiming that because there was a decisive majority at the First Reading, opposition arguments during the Second Reading were diminished by that result. But Shore rejected Rippon's claim on the grounds that the debate on the first reading was held in ignorance. This was because vital documents were not then available to parliamentarians, the First Reading was only Parliament's authorisation to continue negotiations and to enable detailed examination of the consequences of membership of the EEC to be studied and understood.

The Second Reading debate was long and bitter and resulted in the narrow victory for the Government already described.

The greater part of Hansard's[11] pages chronicling the debate can be accessed in the CD: 'Shoe-horned into the EU'[12]. The following are some of the more important speeches taken from that record[13]. They stand on their own merit or lack of merit, generally requiring no amplification or commentary:

---

[8] Hansard column numbers are added after each speaker's name to facilitate those readers wishing to look up the written record.

[9] Treaty of Accession.

[10] Treaty of Luxembourg.

[11] The Parliamentary record.

[12] Available from the author.

[13] Hansard column numbers are added after each speaker's name to facilitate those readers wishing to look up the written record.

Geoffrey Rippon (Col. 279), Chancellor of the Duchy of Lancaster, moving the motion, assured the House that "*... no Parliament can preclude its successors from changing the law*".

Enoch Powell (Col. 283), questioned the value of Rippon's reassurance, and asked: "*why* [then] *is there any doubt that has to be removed by those words that Parliament can subsequently alter what it has already passed*" necessitating the qualifying clause: "*except as may be provided by any act passed after this act* [ECA72]"[14] to be added, in referring to Rippon's statement that Community law takes precedence. <u>An answer was never provided</u>.

Peter Shore (Col. 288), for the opposition complained that the House had only had access to the Treaties, which the Communities had entered into, one week before [the debate].

Peter Shore went on: "*we are to have imposed upon us a written constitution, a constitution that we did not write or did not even help to write*".

Peter Shore (Col. 301), "*When the people feel they are being made subject to laws in which they feel they have played no part and taxes to which they have never consented, respect for both law and government is undermined. Our tradition for order and peaceful change is based not only on the character of our own people but on an enduring, if tacit, bargain between Government and governed that the former will play fair and will be scrupulous in how they deal with the people's rights. But if Governments do not play fair, if they behave in a way people consider to be in itself unconstitutional, there is evidence enough in British history to show we are not a docile people but a very determined and fierce one indeed.*"

Bert Oram (Col. 308), "*I think he* [referring to the previous speaker, Dodds-Parker] *will find as this three day debate proceeds that many of us*

---

[14] OFFICIAL REPORT, House of Lords, 8th May, 1967; Vol.282; c.1202 quoted by Rippon in Col. 279. This exception is significant in that it means Parliament can change the law to preclude its successor from changing the law – a bit of a conundrum which Mr. Powell seems to have detected. Whether the House of Lords' REPORT is right or not, is another question that needs clarification, but if correct then Rippon was misleading the House about no Parliament can preclude its successor from changing the law. This is important and needs more research.

will wish to see it conducted not in the way he suggested, but in a much wider context, particularly in the context of the Government's whole approach to the Treaty of Accession and its consequences and the way in which the Government has disregarded what we consider to be the proper rights of Parliament to examine the whole question of British entry."

Note: The 2nd Reading was allocated only 3 days, whereas the preliminary less important, 1st Reading, was given 6 days.

Peter Hordern (Col. 327), *"That is why I take very seriously my right hon, Friend the Prime Minister's assurance that no country's vital interests would be overruled by other members. I rely on this safeguard and in the practice in the Council of Ministers on the unanimity rule[15]."*

Geoffrey Rippon (Col. 353), *"I said that there would be no essential surrender of sovereignty, and successive speakers from both sides of the House have agreed that there is no essential surrender of sovereignty"* – compare this with FCO 30/1048: 'Sovereignty and the European Communities' written in 1971 with commentary by David Noakes and Richard North (refer to Pt II, Chapter.3).

Sir Elwyn Jones (Col. 457), " .... *the Bill fails to spell out the effect of the directly applicable self-executing provisions of the Bill on our existing law or what encroachments they make on our common law. The whole form of the Bill makes it impossible for us to see the changes required in our English law as a result of the adoption of Community law in their settings so as to enable Parliament to make whatever consequential changes Parliament may think desirable. This represents the fundamental failure and fault of the Bill."*

Nigel Spearing (Col. 485), *"Had hon. Gentleman opposite* [Geoffrey Rippon] *thought that the price worth paying and that it was important enough to have democratic institutions inside the Community, we might have been prepared to pay the price: but they have not negotiated it. I think that has been one of the greatest mistakes of any Government or Party at any time in our history, because the idea of parliamentary government and*

---

[15] The unanimity rule which gave nations a veto, was swept away when qualified majority voting was introduced with the Single European Act in 1986.

of democracy is based, as I understand it, on confidence, consent and credibility. People will only do things under the law if they have confidence in the way the law is made."

Two paragraphs later, Spearing continues: "..................... *four things that this House has. They are consultation before legislation; the redress of grievances before granting Supply; representation before taxation; and the responsibility of the Executive. I submit that on all these four things the Government are selling out almost completely."*

Nigel Spearing (Col. 1959, <u>Third</u> Reading)[16], "*The Prime Minister said that the commitment was to negotiate, no more nor less, yet it has transpired that the only negotiations which we have had are negotiations on the transitional period. Anybody reading the Conservative manifesto would not have dreamed that that would be so. If there is a plot[17], it is a plot or an agreement that the Prime Minister knew all the time precisely what the negotiations were going to be about."*

Douglas Jay (Col. 494), "*The speeches which we have so far heard from the Government Front Bench have seemed to me to be designed not so much to defend as to conceal what the Government are doing to Parliament in this Bill."*

Douglas Jay (Col. 499), "*The three other applicant countries are to hold referenda on the question of joining the Community and apparently, rightly in my opinion, the Prime Minister proposes one for Northern Ireland. Nobody pretends that the Government have any mandate for this Bill from the people or anything approaching full-hearted consent. ...... Millions of people in this country will feel as I do, that legislation passed in this way, with no consent, cannot command the assent of the country and would lack moral and constitutional validity."*

---

16 Reference to Spearing's Third Reading speech here, has been included for completeness and to highlight his argument that the Government in its manifesto committed themselves to negotiate the terms of entry but had not done so, only negotiating the terms of the 'transitional period'.

17 This remark refers to a denial by Selwyn Gummer of accusations of a plot made by John Mendelson regarding collusion between the Government and the Press over a mythical Bill.

[MR. JAY.]

Some hon. Members have said in this debate, " Let us get out of this difficulty by forming a directly elected Common Market Parliament with real powers." I appreciate that that is the honestly held view of some people. But it would mean out-and-out federation, and the end of Britain as a sovereign independent country. That may be what some people want but we know that not more than one in a hundred of the British people and not more than a tiny minority in this House really want that. Indeed, if this is what the Prime Minister really wants I wish he would have the honesty to say so.

I find it extraordinary—this is, of course, an issue which is far above and beyond party politics—that any Government with no shred of mandate should even introduce a Bill which is, from any informed point of view, a constitutional outrage.

The three other applicant countries are to hold referenda on the question of joining the Community and apparently, rightly in my opinion, the Prime Minister proposes one for Northern Ireland. Nobody pretends that the Government have any mandate for this Bill from the people or anything approaching full-hearted consent.

The Prime Minister's " sole commitment ", to use his own words from the Conservative Party Manifesto, is to " negotiate—no more, no less ". To press ahead with such a Bill in these circumstance is, in my view, a breach of faith by the Prime Minister as well as a constitutional monstrosity. Millions of people in this country will feel, as I do, that legislation passed in this way, with no consent, cannot command the assent of the country and would lack moral and constitutional validity.

My right hon. Friend the Member for Fulham (Mr. Michael Stewart) said in a recent Irish debate that it was highly dangerous to destroy people's confidence in the constitution and legal processes by which society is held together. I wholeheartedly agree.

If this legislation is passed, the Prime Minister will be not merely undermining the future economy of the nation and our place in the world. He will be damaging—something which has not occurred in Britain in three centuries—, the confidence of the people in the way they are governed and the way in which the laws binding them are passed.

I am at least grateful to the Leader of the House for his agreement two weeks ago that anything done by this Parliament can be undone by the next. If a Measure anything like this were passed by this House, it must be, and it will be, repealed by the next.

But how infinitely better for the House to reject the Bill totally now. If it were to do that, then it would be performing the greatest service to the people of Britain, and winning the most heartfelt applause from them, in the whole of its long history.

7.26 p.m.

Mr. Peter Mills (Torrington): I welcome the opportunity to speak in this important debate. Although I will not comment on most of the points raised by the right hon. Member for Battersea, North (Mr. Jay), I must in fairness point out that he has been consistent in his view on this issue. One must, therefore, respect him for his view, even if one disagrees with it.

I have been somewhat saddened by the attitude of some pro-Marketeers on the benches opposite—particularly, for example, the hon. Member for Midlothian (Mr. Eadie) and the hon. Member for Enfield, East (Mr. Mackie)—because although not an ardent pro-Marketeer, I have been anxious to hear the views of hon. Members on both sides with a view to being influenced by their remarks.

Bearing that in mind, I am bound to be saddened when I hear hon. Members veering away from views they have expressed and held in recent weeks. My general view about the Bill and about going into Europe has not changed. As I say, I am not an ardent pro-Marketeer, though I accept that the economic case for our entry is good. I have political reservations, and from the federal point of view I am still violently opposed, but my overall view, which has not changed fundamentally, is that it will benefit Britain to join the Common Market.

The Bill makes it abundantly clear that there will be changes in many spheres of our national life. Many changes will have to be made to enable us to comply

Douglas Jay - Hansard 16th February 1972, columns 499 and 500

Denzil Davies[18] (Col. 507), " *...the Bill provides that a 100 or more treaties — 10 volumes I am told — will also be incorporated into the law of the United Kingdom. No attempt is made even to list them, let alone list them in this Bill.*"

The Chancellor of the Duchy of Lancaster [Geoffrey Rippon] *tells us there are 1500 regulations, 40 volumes of them. There is no mention of the regulations in the Bill, no listing of them. None is annexed to the Bill.*

The reason is obvious. It is to debar us as far as possible from putting down Amendments so that these treaties, regulations and directives can be properly debated and so that the people who will have to obey them in future can know the law that they are obeying."

" *..... it is another example of of the lengths to which the present Executive is prepared to go to conceal from the public and the House the full effects of joining the European Communities.*"

Neil Marten (Col. 522), "*Then there is the vital matter of the pledge given by the Right hon. Gentleman the Prime Minister during the last election on 2nd June, 1970 and in Paris before then, about not joining the Common Market without the full-hearted consent of Parliament and the people.*"

Neil Marten (Col. 524), "*...But if we proceed on a small majority, the important election pledge given by the Prime Minister on behalf of our Party will have been broken.*"

Neil Marten (Col. 525), "*.... the public will regard politicians rightly with utmost contempt and I am not prepared to condone that.*"

Neil Marten (Col. 527), "*We anti-market Conservatives have had plenty of pressure put upon us[19], not by arguments on the merits of the case for joining but by other means. I believe that by behaving like that, the Conservative Party has harmed the very case that it was trying to make to*

---

18 Denzil Davies, the MP who challenged Margaret Thatcher, PM, over the sinking of the Argentine cruiser, General Belgrano in 1982.

19 Refer to Part II, Chapter. 5., showing the intimidation Neil Marten was subjected to within his Banbury Constituency Association.

us".

James Prior (Col.552), "*I believe the agriculture industry of this country is not only broadly in favour of joining but recognises very well that it has a great opportunity by doing so.*"

Harold Wilson (Col.630), "*We may have these doubts about our ability to pay these bills because of the crippling burden imposed on our balance of payments by the terms negotiated[20].*".

Harold Wilson (Col.638), "*.... There has been virtually no consideration in these papers* [speaking of pro-Market newspapers] *of the rights of Parliament, of the vast constitutional implications ....* "

Harold Wilson (Col. 643), "*In our judicial system, evolved over centuries, the judge does not get involved in a case himself so much as listen to council for and against and then decided independently. That system is to be assimilated much more closely to the French system of law, where the judges are advocates for both sides, are examining juries, and at the end of the day pronounce judgement.*"

Edward Taylor (Col.882), "*I have read in the newspapers of great pressures imposed upon my colleagues.*"

Enoch Powell (Col. 706), "*Let us wrap it up, so that what we are talking about is the full-hearted consent of the House of Commons. There was a debate in October* [first reading] *– a debate which did not deal with a precise proposition such as this – when the House decided affirmatively by a vote of seven twelfths in favour. In no country with a written constitution, in none of the other countries which are participating in this operation with the United Kingdom, would such a proportion justify the major step which is involved in joining the Community. All of them have safeguards which require a much more generous margin even than that on which the House voted on 28th October.*"

---

[20] Note that the economy went into serious decline following entry, resulting in Heath's 3-day week (due to miner's strike and resulting power shortages). Heath then called a general election on the theme, 'who runs Britain?' (meaning the unions or the Government). Ironically, he might well have asked: 'Who runs Britain? – the British Government or Brussels'.

Alfred Morris (Col. 728), " .... *It is suggested that the Prime Minister may say tonight that he will resign if he is unable to carry this Bill. His reason for saying this would be that his European commitments are crucial to his policies as a whole. If he had said that at the General Election, he would have been the vanquished, not the victor. He would not have been the Prime Minister today.*"

Edward Heath, The Prime Minister, makes the vote a confidence motion (Col. 752), "*Therefore if this House will not agree to a second reading of the Bill tonight ...... my colleagues and I are unanimous that in these circumstances this Parliament cannot sensibly continue[21].*"

The motion was passed by 309 votes to 301 votes

Harold Wilson, Leader of the Opposition stated after the result of the vote was announced (Col. 758), "*...in breach of his election promise, the Prime Minister has not got the full hearted consent of the British people. Secondly, he has not got the full-hearted consent of Parliament. Thirdly, when he said that he must get this through on Tory votes in a majority, he has not done so.*"

---

[21] By this statement, Heath was making it a confidence motion – a threat to dissolve Parliament and the calling of a general election should the Bill fail. This threat was meant to play upon the insecurities of MPs who had small majorities.

CHAPTER 12

The Questions then…

The pages of this book give detailed information about the Heath Government's campaign of the early 1970s which took Britain into the then Common Market. It's a story that has only been told in part before.[1] This book has been written to complete the picture, including the background to the picture (see Part.II of this book, following) to tell the full story, so far as it has been documented or still known[2], for the first time.

Was it really in the best interests of Britons, as the public was repeatedly told, to have a foreign order imposed? Was our entry, in the context of moral legitimacy and Britain's written Constitution, legitimate? Was Parliament and its elected representatives subjected to undue pressures, in some instances intense pressures, by a subversive campaign orchestrated by all sorts of vested interests, mainly corporate interests? The answer to the latter question is a definite 'yes', as these pages repeatedly show. Whether there has been any economic benefit to the population at large is up to the reader to judge.

Did Parliament in 1972, and after, by its act of handing parliamentary powers[3] to the unelected and unaccountable Brussels' bureaucracy, put its own legitimacy in doubt?

Hugh Fraser MP, speaking in the Third Reading of the EC Bill on 13th July 1972[4], foresaw the alienation from the electoral process that we see today and the feebleness of government which can do nothing about it, without repatriating powers from Brussels, when

---

[1] Shoe-horned into the EU produced in 2004, was the first known attempt to examine the records from the early 1970s that had been locked away under the 30 year rule by the government and only released to the public in 2003.

[2] Most of the people involved at the time are now dead. Those still living are elderly and either have faded memories or are not telling – some have much to hide.

[3] The Conservative MEP, Nirj Deva had calculated 10 years ago in a 2004 paper (lodged in the House of Commons library), that even then, 65% of our laws were made in Brussels

[4] Column.1941.

he said: "*The history of Parliament over a thousand years has been the way in which the people of this country have been able to participate in the exercise of power. This has taken a thousand years to bring about.*
But I believe that it is certain that by going into Europe we shall see not something which is alien but a true alienation of the British people from the Government and the control of their own interests. That worries me greatly."

Finally, we return to the opening quotation from Douglas Jay MP, *that our membership of the EU* [or EEC as it was then]: "*….lack*[s] *moral and constitutional validity.*"

This writer has met a general response that the public agreed to it all in the referendum. I ask what referendum and the response generally is the referendum after the Bill was passed in Parliament, meaning 1972.

When this error is corrected, the disbelieving response is: are you sure? The authorities have been pretty cute in letting this myth take root, they have had to, otherwise people might realise the basis for the way they are governed is untenable, and then what?

These pages have provided evidence for readers to consider. Answers to these vital questions are needed, they are vital because it affects our present-day attitudes to our membership of the European Union and the way we are governed. Each must come to their conclusion and decide whether there is something that should be done about it, or just accept the bad situation as it is.

This author leaves the reader with one final thought: is it conceivable that the people of this country and our elected representatives would have had truck with joining the EEC if they had been aware of the double dealings that were routinely happening in the period leading up to Britain's entry in 1973? No doubt those involved were secure with the knowledge that documents would be hidden away from public gaze for 30 years and that by the time they saw the light of day again, the country would be locked into federal state called Europe. How it all came about would no longer be of particular interest. Well they were wrong.

PART II

European Integration - the broader picture

1948 -2014

CHAPTER 1

ACUE and the European Movement

The American Committee on United Europe (ACUE) rescued the European Movement (EM) in its infancy, saving them from certain bankruptcy. As we have seen in the Preface, Duncan Sandys and Joseph Retinger travelled to America in October 1948 to seek the necessary funds for its rescue. ACUE together with the CIA essentially controlled the direction the EM and hence European integration took through the 1950s and beyond.

National branches of the European Movement were thereafter rapidly established in every European country outside of the Soviet bloc. The European Movement projected itself as a grass roots organisation, but nothing could have been further from the truth as the ACUE list of financial backers below makes clear.

It's not unfair to state that without the European Movement and its American backers there would be no European Union today – the EM itself claims that credit. Although when asked for a copy of its history, it replies there isn't one[1].

The objectives and names of individuals, corporations and companies listed below are taken from Francois Xavier Rebattet's[2] Thesis (1962)[3] on the origins of the European Movement:

ACUE Statement of Purpose:

A joint 'Statement of Purpose' was issued by the Atlantic Union (AU)[4] and ACUE in 1951, which Statement accommodated their differing approaches (AU looking for a speedier process towards World union) to unity in general and European Unity in particular:

---

[1] That was the experience of this writer – they were not admitting to the Rebattet Thesis.

[2] Francois Rebattet was the son of George Rebattet, Secretary General of the EM after Duncan Sandys was deposed in 1950.

[3] The European Movement 1945 – 1953, Bodleian Library, Oxford.

[4] Clarence Streit, a 'Rhodes' scholar, wrote 'Union Now' and founded the Federal Union. In March 1949, Streit and Owen J. Roberts, former Supreme Court justice, established the Atlantic Union committee. Roberts said he considered national sovereignty a "silly shibboleth". See also the back cover of this book for President Roosevelt on staying out of WWII.

' .... ACUE believes that the integration of Europe politically and economically is a first and essential step; and until that is accomplished, the extension of such integration to other members of the Atlantic community, such as Canada and the United States, should wait for future consideration. AU, on the other hand, believes that integration of Europe does not go far enough to meet the present situation and that only with the inclusion of the United States can a union of democracies achieve a viable economy and sufficient defensive strength to achieve peace.'

It is interesting that this statement anticipated the North Atlantic Free Trade Area (NAFTA) and its successor organisation Trans-Atlantic Investment Partnership (TTIP) that is currently exercising democracy campaigners[5].

The Statement of Purpose projected a powerful message of American intent, but how far it reached into the public psyche at the time, is impossible to ascertain. Anyway, the fact is that Europe went in the direction that America desired, with Britain dutifully tagging along following its drubbing at Suez, with every Prime Minister, excepting Harold Wilson[6], clinging to Uncle Sam's apron strings.

Of course the USA held all the cards, immensely rich and with Europeans in fear of the Soviet Union engendered by the Cold War, were only too willing to comply. This, with aid, with strings attached, from the Marshall Plan[7], was decisive in setting the political direction Europe followed.

Francois Xavier Rebattet tried to make light of American

---

[5] Notably '38 Degrees'.

[6] Wilson managed to avoid getting sucked into the Vietnam War but accused of being on Moscow's payroll as s result – see Peter Wright's book 'Spycatcher'.

[7] The Marshall Plan (named after Secretary of State General George Marshall) was officially known as the 'European Recovery Program'. The USA gave, with strings (which meant there had to be progress towards European integration), $17 billion in economic support to help rebuild European shattered economies after the end of the Second World War. General William Donovan Chairman of ACUE made a speech on 20th December 1949: ' ..... If there are differences among members of of the Committee of Ministers which suggest that some are less prepared than others to make rapid progress to European unity ..... Marshal aid might be substantially curtailed.'

involvement, no doubt influenced by his father, George, the EM's former Secretary General, whose position had depended on it[8].

Membership of ACUE

Rebattet's Thesis provided a description of the membership, which goes a long way to understand its nature, purpose and influence over the European integration process: *'The American Committee .....* [ACUE] *had in 1950 a membership of 380 including its Officers and Directors. If one looks at its membership from the point of view of occupations and sectors of interest, there was a marked predominance of businessmen and bankers with a good number of lawyers, these three categories having a total of 209 representatives. The catering for the support of large firms* [corporations] *answered the major activity of ACUE which was to raise funds for EM. There was a relatively small number of academics: 24 .... The activities known as mass 'media' in America were represented by 29 prominent people in the field. Very few politicians could be found among members .... This was probably due to the fact that ACUE wished to remain as non-political as possible because of its fund-raising activities and its relationship with EM.'*

Firms [corporations][9]:

Harold Boeschenstein, President of Owens-Corning Fibreglass Corp
Henry P. Bristol, President of Bristol-Myers Company
Harry A. Bullis, Chairman of General Mills, Inc
Harvey H. Bundy of Choate
Hall and Stewart
Henry B. Cabot, Director of Samuel Cabot, Inc
Robert L. Clarkson, Chairman of American Express Company
Carle C. Conway, Chairman of Revere Copper and Brass, Inc
M. Hartley, Chairman of Remington Arms Company, Inc
Donald B. Douglas, Chairman of International Mining Corporation
Martin S. Erlanger, Chairman of B.V.D. Corporation

---

[8] Rebattet wrote that the EM rejected the Statement of Purpose, but doesn't explain on what grounds. No doubt the EM would have preferred to have operated independently of the USA, but that was not an option.

[9] The names are all taken from the Thesis.

Henry T. Ewald, President of the Campbell-Ewald Company
W.H. Hoover, President of Anaconda Copper Mining Corp
Philip Cortney, President of Coty, Inc
Amory Houghton, Chairman of Corning Glass Works
C. Mahlon Kline, President of Smith, Kline and French Laboratories
George W. Merck, President of Merck and Company, Inc
Lester E. Jacobi, President of Schenley Distillers Corporation
Erwin C. Uhlein, Jr., President of Joseph Schlitz Brewing Company
George N. Jepperson, Chairman of Norton Company
J.M. Kaplan, President of Welch Grape Juice Company
Meyer Kestnbaum, President of Hart Schaffner and Marx,
William B. Bell, President of Hart, Schaffner and Marx
William B. Bell, President of American Cyanamid
Philip D. Reed, Chairman of General Electric Company
Blaine S. Smith, President of Universal Atlas Cement Company
Spyros Skouras, President of Twentieth Century Fox Film Corporation
J.P. Spang, Jr., President of Gillette safety Razor Company
Cornelius V. Starr, Chairman of American International Underwriters
Walter A. Stewart, President of American Optical Company
George E. Warren, Director of Remington Rand, Inc
Thomas J. Watson, Chairman of International Business Machines Corp [IBM]
H.D. Collier, Chairman of Standard Oil Company of California
H.F. Wilkie, Vice President of Joseph E. Seagram & Sons Inc
And William Zeckendorf, President of Webb & Knapp, Inc

Bankers

(The following were bank managers)
George F. Baker, Jr., Director of First National Bank of New York; Stephen C. Clark, Vice President of the Safe Deposit Company New York; Chester C. Davis, President of the Federal Reserve Bank of St Louis Frederick; W.Gehle and Thomas H. McKittick, Vice Presidents of Chase National Bank; Walter N. Rothschild, President

of Abrahams and Strauss; D.M. Spencer, Chairman of the Fiduciary Trust Company of New York

Lawyers

Among the most important lawyers were:
Chauncey Belknap, of Patterson, Belknap and Webb;
Adolf A. Berle, Jr., of Berle, Agee and Land also former Assistant Secretary of State and Ambassador;
William Adams Delano of Delano and Aldrich;
Sylvan Gotschal of Well; Gotschal and Manges;
and John Foster Dulles of Sullivan and Cromwell

Academics

The most eminent academics were:
Frederick Burchardt, President of Bennington College
Harry Woodburn Chase, Chancellor of New York University
Arthur Schlesinger from Harvard
George N. Schuster, President of Hunter College
and Harrold E. Stassen, President of the University of Pennsylvania

Mass Media

The next important representatives of 'mass-media' on ACUE were:

George Abbott, producer,
Dr. Max Ascoli, publisher of (The Reporter)
James Wright Brown, editor and publisher
Sevellon Brown, published of Providence Journal
Gardener and John Cowles respectively Presidents of Look Magazine and Minneapolis Star and Tribune
Robert Little of the Reader's Digest
Henry R. Luce, Director of Time Inc
Ralph McGill, Editor of the Atlanta Constitution
Malcolm Muir, Publisher of Newsweek
Mrs. HelenRogers Reid, President of the New York Herald Tribune
Geoffrey Parsons, from the same newspaper
H.V. Keltenborn

And two leading advertisers: George R. Katz, President of Katz Agency
and Signard S. Larmon, President of Young and Ribican, Inc

Trade Unions

Trade Unions were also represented by:

William Green, President of AFL

Personalities

There were also the following personalities:

Bernard M. Baruch, Former Chairman of the U.N. Atomic Energy Commission
Harry F. Guggenheim, former Ambassador to Cuba
Paul V. McNutt, Former High Commissioner to the Philipines
Robert Moses, William Phillips, Former Ambassador to Italy
Lewis L, Strauss, Former Member of U.S. Atomic Energy Commission
Myron C. Taylor, Former Representative to the Vatican
James H. Wolf, Chief Justice of the Supreme Court of Utah
Mrs. David Rockefeller
Douglas Fairbanks
John Gunther
Edward Streichen

Politicians

Very few politicians could be found among members of A.C.U.E.:

Representatives:

Hale Boggs
Christain A. Herter
Jacob K. Javits

Senators:

Paul Douglas
J.W. Fulbright
Herbert A. Leman
Brien McMahon

Officers of ACUE

William J. Donovan, Former Director of the Office of Strategic Services

Chairman, Allen W. Dulles, Director of Central Intelligence Agency

Vice Chairman, George S. Franklin, Director of the Council of Foreign Relations [CFR]

Secretary, and Francis Adams Truslow, President of the New York Curb Exchange, Treasurer.

The Board of Directors included:

Thomas W. Braden, Executive Director

David Dubinsky, President of International Ladies Garment Workers of A.F. of L

Aurthur J. Goldberg, General Council of the Congress of Industrial Organisations

Which showed that the trade unionists were not numerous in ACUE, but were represented by some of their leaders:

Charles R. Hook, Chairman of Armco Steel Corporation

Walter N. Maguire, of Maguire, Walker and Middleton

Arnold J. Zurcher, Executive Director of Sloane Foundation

Raymond B. Allen, President of University of Washington

Conrad N. Hilton, President of Hilton Hotels

David E. Lilienthal, Former Chairman of the US Atomic Energy Commission

Lucien D. Clay, Former Commander of the U.S. Forces in Germany and Lieutenant General Walter Bedell Smith, Commanding General of the First Army.

By 1951, ACUE had increased its membership by 217 bringing it to almost 600.

Its leadership shared by leading businessmen and members of the CIA or of the State Department largely determined its types of activity.

Successors to General Donovan (who died in 1958) at the head of

ACUE were:

Paul G. Hoffmanand, and later William C. Foster, both former administrators to ECA [Economic Co-operation Organisation].

Allen Dulles was replaced as Vice-Chairman by Paul G. Hoffman and Francis A. Adams Trustlow as Treasurer by Mrs. John J. McCloy.

Comment:

Considering the above corporate list, it is difficult not to conclude that the United States had an almost decisive effect upon the course of European history leading to the present European Union following WWII. In addition, the United States had a huge military presence on Western European soil, which together with Marshall Aid, meant influence through the dependence it brought, not to mention the social interaction that would have taken place[10].

Brief histories of some of the Corporations (full list above) supporting ACUE

Samuel Cabot Inc. Manufacturer of wood stains and surface preparation products, mostly for exterior use.

During World War II, Cabot developed a black-out paint, used to darken windows to reduce their visibility to German war planes, which was mainly sold to U.S. government agencies. In October 1944 Cabot II patented a method of reducing the visibility of an object when seen against the sky, water or distant background. Sales increased every year from 1942 through 1954.

Merck & Co. traces its origins to Darmstadt, Germany in 1668; and Emanuel Merck who took over the store several generations later, gradually built up a chemical-pharmaceutical factory that produced pharmaceutical preparations and a multitude of other chemicals.

---

[10] Not unsurprisingly, there was resentment from such dependence, especially in France. This was one of the stated reasons for forming Bilderberg in 1952. And in 1966, French President General de Gaulle told NATO to remove its two principal HQs from French territory as he no longer saw a need for NATO. NATO HQ was re-located to Brussels where it remains today.

The company oversaw America's germ-warfare research at Fort Detrick. The US company has about 56,700 employees in 120 countries and 31 factories worldwide. It is one of the top 7 pharmaceutical companies worldwide. In November 2009, Merck merged with Schering-Plough in a US$41 billion deal.

Schlitz Brewing Co. Gained its name in 1858, after a take-over. The company flourished through much of the 1900s, starting in 1902 when the production of 1 million barrels of beer surpassed Pabst's claim as the largest brewery in the world. Schlitz would continuously be in competition as one of the top breweries in America for the next 70 years.

Hartmarx Corporation. Hartmarx a leading men's clothing wholesaler, with over $600 million in annual sales to department stores, catalog companies, and other retailers; its headquarters remained in Chicago, where it employed about 1,000 people.

Remington Rand, Inc. From 1942 to 1945, Remington Rand was one manufacturer of the M1911, A1 .45 calibre automatic pistol used by the United States Armed Forces during World War II. Remington Rand produced more M1911A1 pistols than any other wartime manufacturer.

IBM. Designer and manufacturer of computers, particularly main-frame types, of which the 'Blue Gene' Supercomputer is its latest product. IBM was awarded the National Medal of Technology by President Obama in 2009. Today, one of the oldest and largest corporations in the World, with its headquarters in New York with over 400,000 employees world-wide. Thomas Watson lead IBM for an astounding 42 years until 1956.

When Hitler came to power in 1933, the Nazis set out to identify the Jewish Community through some sort of cross-indexing system. IBM had produced a punch card sorting system and through its German subsidiary Dehomag[11], made Hitler's programme of Jewish

---

[11] Abbreviation for Deutsche Hollerith Maschinen Gesellschaft. 'Hollerith' was the name of the American inventor of the punch card system that gave rise to the machine named after him. Hollerith founded the Tabulating Machine Company, the company that eventually became IBM.

destruction a technological possibility[12]. With the knowledge of New York's IBM HQ, Dehomag, using its own staff and equipment (Hollerith machines) provided the assistance to Hitler's Hollocaust programme. The machines were leased to the German Census Bureau, not sold and the punched cards could only be designed, printed and purchased from IBM — they had the company's name printed on them.

Watson and Hitler met for discussions in 1937, was decorated by

Punched card as used on Hollerith machines used for census purposes

Hitler and 'wined and dined and honoured in Berlin'.

While IBM (through its Dehomag subsidiary), and its Hollerith machines were helping the Nazi regime round up and transport Jews and other 'undesirables' in Germany and the occupied territories, IBM was helping the American war effort at home with Hollerith machines it (through subsidiaries) was manufacturing weapons of war.

The double dealing, although largely ignored by the American bureaucracy, was noticed by a Harold Carter, a Government investigator. He did his utmost to unravel the covert IBM (through Dehomag) German operation. But finally Carter ended up not

---

[12] IBM and the Holocaust, by Edwin Black, recently revised and republished in 2011.

prosecuting IBM, but working with them because he found that they were not to be thought of as a suspect company trading with the enemy, but a vital resource needed for the American war effort.

Standard Oil. A predominant American integrated oil producing, transporting, refining, and marketing company. It was the largest oil refiner in the world and operated one of the world's first and largest multinational corporations until broken up in 1911. John D. Rockefeller was a founder, chairman and major shareholder, he became the the richest man in history.

In 1941, an investigation exposed a 'marriage' cartel between John D. Rockefeller's United States-based Standard Oil and I.G. Farben whose subsidiary produced Zyklon 'B' gas. Standard Oil was accused of complex price and marketing agreements between DuPont, a major investor in and producer of leaded gasoline and other companies. The investigation was eventually dropped due to the need to enlist industry support in the war effort.

IG Farben built a factory for producing synthetic petroleum and rubber (from coal) at Auschwitz. This was the beginning of SS activity and camps at this location during the Holocaust. At its peak in 1944, this factory made use of 83,000 slave labourers. The pesticide Zyklon B, for which IG Farben held the patent, was manufactured by Degesch (Deutsche Gesellschaft für Schädlingsbekämpfung), which IG Farben owned 42.2 percent of (in shares) and which had IG Farben managers in its Managing Committee. Zyklon B was the primary form of gas used throughout WWII in Nazi death camps.

Joseph E. Seagram & Sons. Incoperated as a producer of distilled spirits and wines. Seagram & Sons, Inc. is a subsidiary of Vivendi.

First National Bank of New York. Founded in 1812 as the City Bank of New York, later taken over by Moses Taylor, a protégé of John Jacob Astor and one of the giants of the business world in the 19th century. In 1896, it was the first contributor to the Federal Reserve Bank of New York.

By 1919, the bank had become the first U.S. bank to have billion dollars in assets.

Under its Chairman, E. Mitchell, from 1929, the bank expanded rapidly and by 1930 had 100 branches in 23 countries outside the United States. In 1933 a Senate investigated Mitchell for his part in tens of millions dollars in losses, excessive pay, and tax avoidance. Senator Carter Glass said of him: *"Mitchell more than any 50 men is responsible for this stock crash."*

In 1952, James Stillman Rockefeller was elected president and then chairman in 1959, serving until 1967. Stillman was a direct descendant of the Rockefeller family. In 1960, his second cousin, David Rockefeller[13], became president of Chase Manhattan Bank, National City's long-time New York rival for dominance in the banking industry in America.

The Federal Reserve Bank of St. Louis. One of 12 regional Reserve Banks that, along with the Board of Governors in Washington, D.C., make up the nation's central bank. Missouri is the only state to have two Federal Reserve Banks (Kansas City also has a bank).

The St. Louis Fed. is the headquarters of the Eighth Federal Reserve District, which includes the state of Arkansas and portions of Illinois, Indiana, Kentucky, Mississippi, the eastern half of Missouri, and West Tennessee.

The Chase Manhattan Bank. Formed in 1931 after the purchase of Chase National Bank by the Bank of the Manhattan Company. In August 1914, Henry P. Davison, a Morgan partner, travelled to the UK and made a deal with the Bank of England to make J.P. Morgan & Co. the monopoly underwriter of war bonds for UK and France. The Bank of England became a 'fiscal agent' of J.P. Morgan & Co. and vice versa. The company also invested in the suppliers of war equipment to Britain and France.

---

13 David Rockefeller was prominent in Bilderberg from its inception – see Chapter.8 following.

CHAPTER 2

Consolidation – the meaning of the June 5th 1975 Referendum

The common misunderstanding among the public today is that there *was* a referendum in 1972 where the electorate was supposed to have consented to joining the European Economic Community (EEC) following ECA(72)[1] passing through parliament. This misconception suited the establishment well as they hope it (the misconception) provided cover for the questionable campaign conducted by the Government in 1970/72[2].

There was a referendum on the EEC of course, but that was in 1975 and was a post-legislative, non-binding, retrospective referendum[3], some 2½ years after entry. The 1975 referendum was conducted to approve the country's continued membership of the EEC, sometimes described as the Common Market at the time, joined on January 1st, 1973.

Others, unaware of the fact, have wondered why there wasn't a referendum before ECA(72) passed through Parliament, as should have occurred for such a constitutional change. But the simple answer was, that prior to 'going in', there was just not enough support[4] for the Government to win a referendum. The Government, if it had agreed to a referendum, might also have been forced to agree to equal funding for both sides. As it was, the private campaign against was deliberately refused funds, whilst the Government's campaign was massively funded from corporate sources, taxpayer's money (via the civil service), and, which was not public knowledge at the time, the American CIA.

---

[1] European Communities Act 1972)
[2] See Part.I.
[3] Post legislative referendum meaning that the public are retrospectively asked to approve something the government had done, in this instance, 2 ½ years earlier.
[4] Poll of polls showed just 18% in favour in January 1971.

In Pt.I, Chapter.10, 'Resisting a Referendum', showed there *was* in fact demand for a referendum, with the campaign for one headed by Tony Benn. Advocates for one came in for abuse, being denounced as 'anti-parliamentary' and 'un-British', and was unnecessary because, it was falsely claimed, 'no loss of sovereignty' was involved.

These establishment arguments (against a referendum) somehow no longer applied when it came to the 1975 Referendum to ratify ECA(72) retrospectively – could that have been because conditions were so much more favourable to the Government (Harold Wilson's) that they expected they could win? They also held an advantage by then because the electorate were being asked to approve the 'status quo', which advantage they hadn't enjoyed in 1972. This fact, and that a 'Yes' answer for continued membership gave the Government, it is, estimated, a 10% head-start over a 'No', was indicative of how unacceptably unfair the Referendum was.

It was said at the time that the referendum was needed because of divisions over Europe within the Labour Party, whose rank and file were incensed at the way the ECA(72) campaign had been conducted. Douglas Jay MP, as we have seen in Part I of this book and it is repeated here for emphasis, said in the House of Commons:

"Millions of people in this country will feel as I do, that legislation passed in this way, with no consent, cannot command the assent of the country and would lack moral and constitutional validity".

Although to some extent this was the case (Labour Party divisions[5]), the real reason was to consolidate the 'gains' made in 1972 – Roy Jenkins, Home Secretary[6] and an ardent europhile declared after

---

[5] There are always divisions in politics, that's what politics is about after all and there was at the time divisions in Conservative ranks, but Conservative whipping system was more effective.

[6] Jenkins as a young subaltern at the outbreak of WWII, was this writer's uncle's commanding officer. As a result of that experience he held him in low regard, saying that the whole (Royal Artillery) troop had nothing but contempt for him. Instead of properly instructing his men in their role before going to war, Jenkins was more interested in holding political classes for his men. Normally subalterns stay with their troop and lead them in battle – Jenkins never led his men into battle.

just 18% in favour of joining with 70% against[14]. This 372% swing in just 4 years looks highly suspicious to the intelligent observer.

There are, however, some pointers that suggest the referendum may have been rigged:

1. Sir Richard Body MP, one of the campaigners for the 'NO' side, reported that, 'two very Anglophile CIA (unnamed) agents, who *"deplored their country's methods in interfering in the affairs of a good ally"* came to see him. They brought with them papers that showed the CIA had already given the European Movement considerable sums of money to fight the Referendum and that a dedicated federalist, Cord Meyer[15] Jnr, was to be head of CIA station in London for the duration of the Referendum. Sir Richard was unable to find a single British newspaper to publish his account or to examine the documents. In the end Body was able to publish the story in *Time Out* magazine – at that time still a small-circulation publication and not one that carried weight with the establishment or public opinion'.

One would hesitate to reproduce this account without some corroborating evidence, of its authenticity. Support, however, is available. Sir Richard's report is consistent with the researches of Dr Richard Aldrich of the Department of Politics at Nottingham University. In his book *The Hidden Hand*, first published in 2001 by John Murray, Aldrich wrote: 'whilst researching CIA activities in Europe, he stumbled across an archive of CIA front organizations in Georgetown University, Washington'.

The documents revealed that millions of dollars had been funneled into Europe, with some into the UK. Aldrich also discovered related correspondence including letters from British MPs'.

These records demonstrated that ACUE, see Pt II, Chapter.1, of this book was, in addition to providing corporate funding to the

---

[14] Refer to Part I, Chapter.11, of this book.
[15] Meyer, once one of the leading figures in the 'United World Federalists', was sent to London as CIA Station Chief from early 1975 until early 1976, a period coinciding with the Referendum campaign – was it just co-incidence that a world federalist became the Station Chief at that critical time?

European Movement was also itself passing on CIA money to them[16].

2. Centralizing the counting was an unusual, if not bizarre decision. It involved complex logistics, presenting opportunities for wholesale electoral fraud. The Liberals in the House of Commons

1975 Referendum count Earls Court 6th June

had wanted the count to be held at constituency level[17], as did the House of Lords, but the government, as governments usually do, got their way, and the prospect for proper scrutiny never materialized.

---

[16] Refer to this book's 'Bibliography' for extracts from Dr Aldrich's book.

[17] As was always the case for local, House of Commons and EU Parliamentary elections.

Detailed scrutiny of ballot papers normally provided by local constituency counts was lost and the 'No' campaign was unable to scrutinize the results nationally. In addition the tallying of ballot papers was conducted by volunteers. This author tried to find out how these volunteers were selected, but has been unable to locate any sources that can answer this important question.

After the referendum the ballot papers were destroyed, but this writer gathers that the original tally is still held in Cabinet Office files. That there is much uncertainty about the 1975 referendum and its legitimacy is a subject that needs researching.

Of course, people would say they wouldn't do that (rig the Referendum) would they? The answer to that question is for the reader to decide.

The main chapters of this book demonstrated that the establishment who ran the country at the time, not only refused a referendum on ECA(72) in 1972 when it should have been held, but had utter contempt for playing fair with the public.

Holding a non-binding referendum 2½ years late was not a concession to popular demand, or a device to close a so-called rift within the Labour Party, but a cynical, contrived ploy to ensure an opposition free period of 10 or 20 years to complete the abolition of Britain as an independent nation-state. The means justified the ends, as they say.

Anecdotal Support

Whilst this cannot of course be considered valid evidence of a fraudulent referendum, it's quite common to hear people who voted in the 1975 referendum say that they didn't know anyone who voted to remain in the, then, EEC. This is not surprising considering the low polling results for the 'YES' side in the period leading up to the adoption of ECA(72) in Parliament and the period up to the 1975 Referendum – here are some comments from web-sites:

'I voted to come out in 1975, my views have not changed. Yes I do think that vote was rigged. Victor

'Yes Victor, I too voted to come out and could not believe the results coming over the television. Toxteth

' ....yes, Brixton...yes....Lambeth....yes....and so on and on until a tiny hamlet with 200 people said no !! The Russian Pravda newspaper said they couldn't have done it better. Then years later it was revealed that anybody on the register that had not voted was counted as a Yes vote[18]. The people have been truly conned. Cameron is a Liar, he has lied once ...he will again. Ukip for me methinks.

'I remember that British Forces and families in Germany had just handed in their voting papers when the 'yes' result was announced, I remember discussing with others "how is that possible when our votes have yet to be flown to UK?"

'We heard that Forces in Cyprus experienced the same thing, but we need some senior officers to come out and confirm these facts and stand up to their political masters .... Kate.

The 'what if' conundrum

Just suppose it were proven beyond any reasonable doubt that the 1975 referendum was rigged to get the 'Yes' result, what would be the constitutional position? Would the UK's membership of the EU be instantly terminated without the application of Article 50[19] of the Lisbon Treaty being applicable?

Unfortunately 'No', because a 'No' referendum result would be non-binding under the terms of the Referendum Act that set the Referendum in motion and the question of leaving the EU or not would be for Parliament to debate and decide. The country would be in the hands of Party whips.

In other words the 1975 Referendum was just a contrivance. The

---

[18] Whether there is any truth in this is an open question that needs researching.

[19] Article.50, part of the EU's Lisbon Treaty, comprise the rules applicable to member states applying to leave the EU.

Government was in a win-win situation. If it lost things would continue as before. If it won, as it did, the matter was settled for a generation or more and integration could proceed virtually unopposed, as it did.

Finally, could there be a relationship between MP, David Steel's speech in the Commons that 'we' *never learned how the Earl's Court count was conducted* and the revelation that it (the Referendum) was organized and conducted by the Americans[20] – could that be CIA Station Chief, Cord Meyer? There were 50,000 ballot boxes carted from every corner of the country to Earls Court in London and/or regional centres[21], yet no one parliamentarian admitted to having the faintest idea of how and to where all those boxes were transshipped.

If an American agency was entrusted with the task, who was it, was it an agency working for the CIA? Could they have had access to boxes while they were in the 3 or 4 day transit period or whilst in storage? If so, an agent would have had no difficulty losing votes or more simply stuffing boxes with extra votes without being detected.

But it was not as though parliamentarians were unconcerned about the minutia of the count, including transportation of ballot boxes – they were:

Alexander Fletcher MP, for instance, speaking in the House of Commons debate on the Conduct of Referendum Bill debate on 23rd April 1975 said:

I think that the most absurd aspect of the referendum is the national count. There is no precedent for it, and it fills me with horror at the prospect of what might go wrong from the possibility of a student prank as thousands of ballot boxes trundle towards London, to the prospect of a recount.

David Steel MP, was also concerned, speaking on the same day:

Presumably arrangements must be made for the ballot boxes to be brought to Earls Court from polling stations throughout the United Kingdom, and

---

[20] The informant does not want their name made public.
[21] Nobody seems to know which.

for the votes to be piled high and counted. The mind boggles at such an exercise, but no doubt plans have been made for it to be done, and we should like to hear about them. It will be a cumbersome process, and it must be expensive. The Committee is entitled to know how much of the £9 million cost is earmarked for this proposed method of count.

and later on that day Steel said in the Commons:

'....... we should amend the [Referendum] *Bill so that we have a local* [constituency] *count instead of the cumbersome procedure suggested by the Government.'*

The following day of the debate, 24th April, Steel resumed his theme complaining that no one knew what was happening and how Parliament itself was kept in the dark about the Earls Court count:

'I have one tiny regret in this matter. It is that in the course of yesterday's debate we never did learn from the right hon. Gentleman how the Earls Court escapade was to be conducted. We never learned, and no doubt we never shall. That will go down as one of the great "might have beens" in British constitutional history.'

Labour MP, Roderick MacFarquhar, fittingly described the referendum arrangements as a: *'psephological grotesquerie, ... an event which would turn London into the confetti capital of the Western World'*.

There was much in the same vein, and it was clear MPs were worried, but no answers were forthcoming from the Government.

The campaign itself was one-sided, the 'NO' side being grossly under-funded. The result was predictable and Sir Richard Body campaigning for a 'No' vote told this writer that he, and the few other MPs travelling the country making speeches were so exhausted that scrutinizing the movement of ballot boxes and attending the count was out of the question. He also said that the lack of funding for their side, left him reduced to beggarly finding the money for his side's expenses.

The National Counting Officer

(The title suggests centralised counting)

Roy Jenkins[22] as Home Secretary at the time, had responsibility for appointing a Chief National Counting Officer[23].

He chose a retired Home Office Permanent Secretary, Lord Allen of Abbeydale, whom he appointed to the post in February 1975 – just three months before the Referendum. Lord Allen, in the tradition of the talented British amateur, had no experience of running elections[24] and no one else had any experience of organizing a referendum, one where everything was to be centralized.

It seems, by his own admission that the organization was, not unsurprisingly, chaotic. Ballot boxes (50,000 of them) would be brought to railway stations and special trains were laid on to bring them to London and then fleets of lorries ferry them to Earls Court.

By the end of April Lord Allen scrapped his plans because he was told there was to be a regional count, as well as one at Earls Court. So the planning had to begin again with just 5 week to go. There was no hope of doing it properly – it takes a whole year planning local elections to get those right.

What a wonderful opportunity to have the result fixed if someone had a mind to do it. If it was (fixed) then was chaos part of the plan to make it easier?

Since 1975, little has been spoken or written of the event; no record

---

[22] Robin Ramsay published an article in Lobster Magazine adapted from a talk he gave in 1996 entitled: 'The influence of intelligence services on the British left'. In this, he categorizing the late Roy Jenkins as belonging to what he described as the 'American [corporate] tendency, (square brackets added by this writer) which he became leader of in 1963, following the death of Hugh Gaitskell. Ramsay claimed 900 British managers and trade unionists travelled to America in the 1950s under the auspices of the 'Anglo-American Council on Productivity', as part of the American effort to 'influence their thinking and decisions in directions *compatible with American goals*', of which European federalism was a major part. It may perhaps be relevant that Lord Allen of Abbeydale, when simply Allen Philips, stayed in the United States from 1950-1952, although as a Commonwealth Fund scholar, but he was clearly a man in the same mould as Jenkins.

[23] Perhaps 'National Returning Officer' would have been a more appropriate title..

[24] He had spent his life working in police, justice and prison matters.

of an audit, no accounting for the ballot boxes, although it is said that count details are still held in a Cabinet office file, but the ballot papers themselves have been destroyed.

But whether or not deliberate foul play was involved, it is not possible to claim the 1975 Referendum was fair and transparent. Which can only mean that the Referendum was not a referendum and added no legitimacy whatsoever to an already illegitimate situation.

CHAPTER 3

FCO 30/1048: The Heath Government knew it would lead to loss of sovereignty

Note: Some of the paragraphs below are reprinted with the permission of David Noakes.

The Foreign and Commonwealth Office (FCO) file: FCO 30/1048 dated June 1971, contains 224 pages relating to the 'Legal and Constitutional implications of United Kingdom joining the EEC'.

The file contains two 'main' Papers by FCO official Denis Greenhill addressed to the Secretary of State (Chancellor of Duchy of Lancaster), Geoffrey Rippon[1], under the heading 'Sovereignty and the European Communities'. The file also contains various other documents including drafting papers, letters, questions and briefings for Parliament, questions about the talks[2] with President Pompidou of France, written answers for the House of Commons, newspaper cuttings and much else.

There is also a draft 'Factsheet on Sovereignty' prepared for the pro-Common Market 'Britain in Europe', an off-shoot of the European Movement, both of which organisations were closely collaborating with the Government[3] during the campaign. The Factsheet was destined for public distribution and is not unsurprisingly, at odds with the briefing provided senior Government ministers in the above mentioned (2) main Papers.

The first 'main' Paper consists of 26 clauses and was described as a Planning Paper[4], and the second, 10 clauses , was a briefer version based upon the first and intended for wider distribution within

---

[1] Geoffry Rippon headed the 'negotiating team' in Brussels.

[2] 20th and 21st May 1971.

[3] The National Archive at Kew has many documents showing government funding for campaigning and is described elsewhere in this book.

[4] Did that mean planning how to keep the truth from the public?

Government circles.

Full discussion of the material in the file is well beyond the scope of this book, but the documents together, provide a broad view of Government and official's thinking at the time and is surely worthy of deeper study[5].

This originally classified Government document remained secret until 2001 when it was released to the Public Record Office at Kew under the 30 year rule which kept documents out of the public domain, including from politicians, until no doubt, it was expected it would no longer matter.

In short, the file shows that the Heath Government was made fully aware of the consequences of enacting the Bill, ECA(72) and that it would lead to a loss of sovereignty and democracy and was therefore treasonable[6]. The FCO 30/1048 analysis provided a stunningly accurate image of the future that joining the EEC would entail. It shows that they were fully expecting Britain to effectively cease to exist as a self-governing, independent state by the turn of the century (1999/2000).

The sponsors of the documents had clear intent – to conceal the loss of sovereignty involved from the politicians who would be voting on the Bill, ECA(72) a few months later, on 28th October. Had these findings on sovereignty been revealed publicly at the time, as they should have been, is it conceivable that ECA(72) would not have been confined to the dustbin of history?

Geoffrey Rippon who, as we see above, was fully acquainted with the the effects upon sovereignty when he introduced the motion to Parliament on the 15th February 1972 – the Bill's Second and main reading, stated: *"there would be no essential surrender of sovereignty…"*.

This mantra, in one form or another, was repeated throughout the public campaign and debates in Parliament.

Here are just a few of the damning clauses in these two Papers:

---

[5] The writer retains a complete copy of FCO 30/1048.
[6] The opinion of David Noakes.

Withering of democratic accountability

Brief -10. *British officials, like those of other member states will necessarily play a more political role over wider areas of public business. The task will be to adapt democratic institutions both in the UK and in Brussels to meet and reduce the real and substantial public anxieties over national identity and alienation from government ....*

Author's Comment:

'British officials, like those of other member states will necessarily play a more political role over wider areas of public business.'

No doubt this prospect was a major factor in the Heath government's success in gaining the collaboration of civil servants

Parliament controlled

Main-1. *Membership of the Communities will involve us in extensive limitations upon our freedom of action.*

For the first time Parliament is binding its successors[7].

Increasing loss of sovereignty

The loss of external sovereignty will however increase as the Community develops, according to the intention of the preamble to the Treaty of Rome "to establish the foundations of an ever closer union among the European peoples ".

Britain's law will be subservient

Main-2. *(iii) The power of the European Court to consider the extent to which a UK statute is compatible with Community Law will indirectly involve an innovation for us, as the European Court's decisions will be binding on our courts which might then have to rule on the validity or applicability of the United Kingdom statute.*

The writ of a foreign power is not allowed under the British Constitution, which convention Heath was breaking.

---

[7] This subject is addressed in more detail in Pt.I, Chapter.11, Parliamentary 'Stitch-up', Footnote.14, yet this argument has not been fully played out

Predicting monetary and military union

Main-18. .... *but it will be in the British interest after accession to encourage the development of the Community toward an effectively harmonised economic, fiscal and monetary system and a fairly closely coordinated and consistent foreign and defence policy. If it came to do so then essential aspects of sovereignty both internal and external would indeed increasingly be transferred to the Community itself.*

No withdrawal, sovereignty diminished

Main-22. *Even with the most dramatic development of the Community the major member states can hardly lose the "last resort" ability to withdraw in much less than three decades. The Community's development could produce before then a period in which the political practicability of withdrawal was doubtful. If the point should ever be reached at which inability to renounce the Treaty (and with it the degeneration of the national institutions which could opt for such a policy) as clear, then sovereignty, external, parliamentary and practical would indeed be diminished.*

Disinformation

Main-24 (i). *After entry there would be a major responsibility on HMG and on all political parties not to exacerbate public concern by attributing unpopular measures or unfavourable economic developments to the remote and unmanageable workings of the Community.*

In other words the UK government was to take the blame for things European.

Transfer of the Executive

Main-24 (ii). *The transfer of major executive responsibilities to the bureaucratic Commission in Brussels will exacerbate popular feeling of alienation from government.*

As has happened, which was no doubt part of the plan.

Erosion of sovereignty

Main-24 (v). *...the more the Community is developed ... the more*

Parliamentary sovereignty will be eroded. …The right … to withdraw will remain for a very considerable time. …The sovereignty of the State will surely remain unchallenged for this century at least.

Ironically, the legitimacy of 'European Rule' of the UK is constantly challenged.

The EU Bureaucracy will rule

Main-25. *The impact of entry upon sovereignty is closely related to the blurring of distinctions between domestic political and foreign affairs, to the greater political responsibility of the bureaucracy of the Community and the lack of effective democratic control.*

'Lack of effective democratic control', i.e. power removed from the people we have seen has been deliberate.

Main-26. [Commentary by Dr. Richard North] *To play an effective part in the Community, British Members of the Commission and their staffs and British officials as negotiators will necessarily assume more political roles than is traditional in the UK. The Community, if we are to benefit to the full, will develop wider powers and coordinate and manage policy over wider areas of public business.*

While other measures are foreseen to eliminate the vestigial influence of the national Parliament:

To control and supervise this process it will be necessary to strengthen the democratic organisation of the Community with consequent decline of the primacy and prestige of the national parliaments.

Finally, and chillingly, these civil servants applaud the process. They know what they have to do:

The task will not be to arrest this process, since to do so would be to put considerations of formal sovereignty before effective influence and power, but to adapt institutions and policies both in the UK and in Brussels to meet and reduce the real and substantial public anxieties over national identity and alienation from government, fear of change and loss of control over their fate which are aroused by talk of the "loss of sovereignty".

And to think we were told by the Heath government that entry to the "Common Market" would involve "no essential loss of sovereignty". Liars they are all.

The Government official authoring the above document had a precise understanding of the future in 'Europe', as those now suffering the effects can well see. These officials welcomed the power and prestige, with limited accountability, the new method of governance would bring.

The Annex to the main Paper, below, shows better than anything the emasculation of Parliamentary powers once the Treaty of Rome had been adopted by passing ECA(72).

ANNEX TO MAIN PAPER

AREAS OF POLICY IN WHICH PARLIAMENTARY
FREEDOM TO LEGISLATE WILL BE AFFECTED BY ENTRY
INTO THE EUROPEAN COMMUNITIES.

1. In general it should he noted that there are very few if any areas in which Parliament will be <u>wholly</u> incapable of action or in which Parliament will be <u>wholly</u> free from restraint. It should also be noted that the boundaries which distinguish these areas are changing all the time, as Community policies develop.

2. Much depends upon the way in which the Community has taken action in any particular area. In the case of action by way of Regulation there is, once the Regulation has been made, no room for Parliamentary action (other than, possibly, to supplement the Regulation or mere debate). Generally speaking Parliament must take the Regulation as it stands, and while with Regulations made by the Council, a United Kingdom Minister (who is subject of course to Parliamentary pressure) will take part in the proceedings leading up to adoption of this Regulation, this is not the case with Regulations made by the Commission. Regulations made by the Commission are however essentially of an implementing rather than policy-making nature. Community action by way of a Directive leaves Parliament freedom of choice as to means but no

freedom as to the result to be achieved. A <u>Recommendation</u> leaves Parliament free to decide not only on the means, but also upon whether to comply with the Recommendation at all.

3. Given these major qualifications, the lists below, which are by no means exhaustive, identify the areas of legislative action which will be principally affected and those which will not.

Customs duties and all other matters incidental to the formation of a customs union:
Agriculture;
Free movement of labour, services and capital;
Transport;
Monopolies and restrictive practices;
State aid for Industry;
Coal and Steel;
Nuclear energy industry;
Company Law;
Insurance Law;
Value added tax;
Social Security for migrant workers.

AREAS IN WHICH PARLIAMENT'S FREEDOM OF LEGISLATIVE ACTION WILL NOT BE SIGNIFICANTLY RESTRAINED

The general principles of criminal law; The general principles of' the law of the contract; The general principles of the law of civil wrongs (tort); Land Law; Relations of landlord and tenant; Housing and town and country planning law; Matrimonial and family law; The law of inheritance; Nationality Law; Trusts; Social services (other than for migrant workers); Education; Health; Local government; Rates of Direct Taxation.

CHAPTER. 4

Pressure in constituencies – Neil Marten MP

This book shows how the Government campaign in the early 1970s was targeted at the British public in a most underhand manner. The campaign used huge amounts of money, some of it from corporate entities. The civil service, suborned by Norman Reddaway, Brussels, then a foreign agency, the European Movement[1] (a corporate asset), and much more as we have seen, were all involved.

MPs who had expressed misgivings, or outright opposition to joining the EEC, were individually singled out for 'treatment'. The unacceptable pressure applied is described in Pt.I, Chapter 11: 'The Parliamentary Stitch-up', under sub-section: 'Whip's Report – pressure on Conservative elected representatives'.

In that chapter we saw how Teddy Taylor MP[2] was persuaded by Heath with the threat of loss of office to change his voting intentions at the Second Reading of the Bill to approve ECA(72). This Chapter has been included to show the effect of the pressure upon those subjected to it, in this instance, Neil Marten.

Neil Marten MP for Banbury

Neil Marten had been MP for Banbury since 1959, which Constituency then included Witney, the seat of Prime Minister David Cameron. He had served with distinction during WWII, firstly in the Royal Armoured Corps, and then with Special Forces. In 1944 he parachuted into France to work with the French

---

[1] The European Movement attended most if not all government planning meetings and then went on to implement what was agreed they should do.

[2] Later Sir Teddy Taylor.

Resistance in preparation for D-Day, being awarded the Croix de Guerre three times. He was also awarded the Norwegian War Medal – a distinguished record indeed.

The Conservatives won the June 1970 election on the assurance that Heath would not take Britain into the Common Market without the "whole-hearted consent of Parliament and the people". Marten had been re-selected the month before to represent Banbury for that election having been proposed by the Association Chairman, Jack Friswell. Among the 200 members present at the re-selection meeting there was not a single dissenting voice. The local press, who were in attendance, reported that his 'anti-Common Market' stand brought 'spontaneous applause', and that he 'received massive support from Party workers'. He went on to hold his seat with a substantial majority of 11,564 votes.

The first reading of ECA(72) was debated from 21st to 28th October 1971 and saw Marten holding firmly to the position he took at his association selection meeting and during the June election campaign, voting, of course, against the Bill.

Marten had in fact been the main protagonist for the Conservative 'No' side and been campaigning alongside Peter Shore (Labour), Tony Benn (Labour), Douglas Jay (Labour), Richard Body (Conservative), Enoch Powell (Conservative) and others.

Marten explained his stance on the Bill:

"In the Conservative Party, we fully recognise that there are some members who hold an opposite point of view to the European Policy; very often on grounds of principle, they take the view that they would not wish to become a member of the EEC. Now, of course, these people would be absolutely free to vote in the way they so decide. This is always the case in the party."

Marten also supported the constitutional position enunciated by the MP Edmund Burke to Bristol electors in 1774:

"An MP's ..... opinion, ... judgement, ... conscience, he ought not to sacrifice to you (the constituents) .... Your representative owes

you not only his industry but his judgement; and betrays you, instead of serving you, if he sacrifices it to your opinion."

Having been granted a mandate by his Constituency Association including its Chairman, *and* a large majority from the electorate at the 1970 election, the Chairman reacted, perhaps under pressure himself, by resigning his position because, in Marten's words: *'because I opposed entry into the Common Market'*. Was this orchestrated by the whips or perhaps Norman St John-Stevas[3]?

Neil wrote later of the Chairman's resignation in a report to the Finance and General Purposes Committee Meeting of 19th October 1970:

'For three years prior to the election (and particularly after I voted in the Commons in 1967 against entry) neither my secretary or I can recall having received a single letter from a constituent objecting to my views. Since the election I have received none; nor has anyone asked me about my voting intentions (except the Chairman and President). From time to time a few constituents have in conversation expressed a contrary view to mine and we have discussed the pros and cons of the issue.'

'I was therefore surprised to learn after the Election that the Chairman had resigned because I opposed entry into the Common Market. In my view, having proposed me for adoption in the full knowledge of my views and in the belief that we would win the election, he should have been prepared to accept the logical consequences. However, as he has now de-resigned, that is of little consequence.'

But that was not all. Marten was asked to desist from actively campaigning against joining the Common Market:

'I was, however, even more surprised when I was requested to desist from actively campaigning against joining the Common market'.

In the next paragraph he was impelled to write:

---

[3] St John Stevas wrote the following year in: 'Third Report and Analysis on the State of the Party on the Common Market Issue' on 1st August 1971; refer to Pt.I, Chapter.11, 'The Parliamentary 'Stitch-up': *'Neil Marten for example, is under very strong pressure from his constituents ….'*. 'His constituents', in reality, meant the Association Chairman and President.

'I was again surprised to be asked to "accept the whip" if it comes to a vote, i.e. to vote in favour of entry. Having just been returned in the General Election, where I said time and time again that I was opposed to entry, it seemed to me that I was being invited to go back on what I had told my electors. I feel I would be less than frank with the F. & G.P. if I did not disclose my deep sense of shock at this request. I only mention this because it seems to me that I am still being urged to overlook my own beliefs and principles, and vote in favour of entry.'

No wonder Norman St John-Stevas, could declare to PM, Edward Heath, that: *"Neil Marten, for example, is under very strong pressure from his constituents......".*

In fact Stevas had overstated it, the pressure according to what we have seen above, seems to have been orchestrated by him via the constituency chairman, certainly not from rank and file membership. It was not so much that they expected Marten to change his position and vote 'YES', clearly the real reason for the pressure was to obstruct him in his role of leadership of 'anti-marketeer', as they liked to put it, Conservatives.

It's hard to imagine the pressure Neil Martin, a man of proven resilience, came under. He didn't buckle, but how many other MPs with less resolve were brow-beaten into submission? We have some idea from Norman Stevas' records, but we can never know the full story. This was not a parliament representing the people, this was not democracy in action, this, taking us into the EEC in 1973, had no real legitimate basis. It reflected a truly squalid period of British history.

Marten's speech at the crucial Second Reading debate to the House of Commons on 16th February 1972, refer to Pt.I, Chapter.11, explaining how he had been pressurized, is repeated here for emphasis[4]:

---

4 No doubt Neil Marten had in mind a particularly unpleasant letter from Conservative Party Central Office in Smith's Square, London, dated 2nd February 1972, just two weeks before he made his speech. In the letter from a John Taylor, Chairman of the Executive Committee, we see a veiled threat of de-selection: *'Rarely as you know, is a MP displaced because of his opinions. The*

"We anti-market Conservatives have had plenty of pressure put upon us, not by arguments on the merits of the case for joining but by other means. I believe that by behaving like that, the Conservative Party has harmed the very case that it was trying to make to us"

So we see those working for the end of Britain as an independent, self-governing, democratic, sovereign nation were not content to have illegal use of the civil service, a sham grass roots, corporate backed, European Movement and corporate media to support them, they had to go further and intimidate and neutralise those campaigning against the hand-over.

Final humiliation

Banbury constituency was ultimately split, with Witney and nearby towns and villages hived off with Neil Marten eased out and his seat taken by Europhile Tony Baldry who (in 2014) was still the incumbent MP. Witney became a constituency in its own right at the 1983 General Election when Douglas Hurd, another Europhile, former diplomat and Edward Heath's former political secretary took the seat for the Conservative Party.

When Hurd retired as MP, Shaun Woodward took his place in a 'holding operation' until David Cameron had 'gained enough experience', with Woodward defecting to New Labour in December 1999 on a contrived pretext. Hurd Protégé, David Cameron, became PPC in March 2000, taking the seat back for the Conservatives at the June 2001 General Election.

David Cameron proved to be every bit as determined about Europe as his mentor – so Neil Marten's spirited battle against EU encroachment was finally purged.

National Union is concerned to elect Conservatives and a Conservative Government, much more than with shades of opinion. The difficulty usually arises with inactivity or neglect and fear that the seat may be lost in consequence. ...... I do not know whether the same effect might be achieved with different words .... '.

CHAPTER 5

85 Frampton Street
(This report was written by the author)

This is Thursday 13th March 2003 and I have had a few hours to reflect on what I have seen and heard last night when I attended Britain in Europe's (B in E) so called 'Spring Reception' at 85 Frampton Street, just off the Edgware Road, London.

Britain in Europe is/was in fact the European Movement with bells and whistles, expensive bells and whistles, metamorphosed for the expected referendum on the European single currency (the euro).

Tony Blair, the Prime Minister, had tipped off powerful corporate interests signalling his intention of abolishing the thousand year old currency and, along with much of Europe, join the euro[1].

Business leaders were to ready themselves again to assemble a fearsome media machine to steer the public, as they had before (in 1972 and 1975), into this novel currency mechanism. The public had already been bombarded with cosy messages telling us that it would be so much easier to compare prices when we crossed the Channel to do our shopping [this event was followed two weeks later by a nicely timed BBC TV programme entitled: 'Evan's Euro Adventure'[2]. The 'Evan' was of course Evan Davis, then the BBC's Economics Editor and presenter of 'Money Programme'. It was flash, it was exciting, it made you want to grab your passport and go and spend some imaginary euros – it looked like the future].

There was however one hurdle for Blair and B in E to cross first – a referendum[3]. To achieve the desired result, we were informed,

---

[1] Those states that did so were effectively ceding control of their economies and leaving it to chance or more powerful forces – is a nation without a currency truly a nation any longer?

[2] The programme concentrated on the advantages for business and featured some catchy and upbeat scenes in an Athen's fruit market. But it did not examine or discuss the costs to the British public of joining the euro. Davis concluded his programme by claiming that if Britain stayed out of the euro, Britain ran "the risk of being excluded from a wonderful single market".

[3] A referendum promise had been extracted by the late Jimmy Goldsmith from all three main parties at the 1997 General election campaign – something that should never be forgotten.

85 Frampton Street

B in E would assemble 400 media and other staff at No. 85 to work to ensure victory in that referendum. Scrapping the pound would, at a stroke, remove one of the main stumbling blocks to Britain's full absorption into the European Union, in the words of the late Hugo Young, *"whether we like it or not"*.

Frampton Street had been deliberately located, in the words of the invitation to the inauguration, *'to be away from the Westminster world and at the heart of our preparations'*, yet 85 Frampton Street had easy access to the BBC Television Centre at nearby Wood Lane where a surfeit of euro-sympathetic presenters could be found. The building, a three story block, had already had the ground floor smartly 'modernised' – fitted out (including wall panelling and false ceiling) as a media centre where, in the words of celebrity speaker, Kenneth Clarke, 'the figures of Government can be wheeled in, in support of the campaign'.

The reception was a stand up affair of, I estimate, some 250 guests (some 95% of whom were male and the majority of those getting on in years[4]), with pretty waitresses serving wine and canapés to this assembly of the great and the good (excepting of course myself), – all 'suits'. I recognised, or noted from lapel badges, several prominent people, Dennis McShane, Europe Minister; Anthony Meyer of Margaret Thatcher 'stalking horse' fame or infamy according to one's point of view; Ian Taylor, Conservative MP, i/c Tory European Network (TEN) and a few other MPs and MP's assistants. Most of the others seemed to be functionaries of one sort or another, or retired. It seemed likely that some of my 250 were B in E staff, either from Central Campaigning Office or from the regions. In spite of the hope expressed in the invitation: 'The objective is to build a genuine grass roots campaign', none of them looked to me to be grass roots sorts. Hardly anyone there looked like they had delivered a leaflet in their life, or had any intentions of doing so.

And of course there was, inevitably, Evan Davis. Davis didn't seem to be there in any media capacity, as it wasn't a media event (no signs of cameras or microphones). Davis would have been a key asset in the B in E's and the Government's campaign, with his air impartiality.

Also present was David Hurford-Jones, Chairman of Oxfordshire's European Movement and also past Chairman of Witney Conservative Association and defector [2003] to New Labour, becoming Chairman of Cotswold Labour Party.

Soon (about 7pm) the evening's speakers were being introduced, first it was Lord Marshall of Knightsbridge, Chairman of British Airways, obviously a good man to have on board, with potential for corporate largesse.

Lord Marshall, didn't have anything ground breaking to tell us excepting that the building we were in was the Campaign Centre

---

4 Like this writer.

for Britain in Europe's effort to sell this country down the drain (no he didn't put it in those terms, but that was what I was thinking). He told us there were regional B in E offices being set up across the country in major cities[5], but didn't identify where, or how many.

Then it was Ken Clarke[6]; Ken was in good form and mildly funny at times, no mumbling this evening, Ken was on a mission. Here are a few of the highlights of the oration:

— the media room would normally be used as a campaigning office but the furniture had been removed for the evening's event.

— the two floors above were part of the facilities.

— Ken asked the audience to help the campaign funds by digging into our pockets before leaving. But I could only assume that this was some sort of cover to make us believe that they weren't awash with the money they clearly were.

— Ken pointedly said that it was no use having all these facilities if there were no grass roots membership available to exploit and/or complement them. Again I wondered whether this was Ken covering up the fact that they don't really care about grass roots, as they were going to depend wholly on the media facilities they had set up and the complicity of the broadcast media and other elements of the press.

— Ken claimed that he had not the faintest idea when a referendum might be held and claimed he had not been able to get into the brain of Tony Blair or Gordon Brown (Chancellor of the Exchequer), but felt sure that, in spite of all reports to the contrary, that Gordon Brown was in truth in favour of Britain joining the single currency [Brown subsequently managed to

---

[5] The cost of 85 Frampton Street and all the regional offices and staff was mind boggling. Had there been equivalent structure and paid help in 1971 and 1975? I thought how could campaigners hope to counter such corporate power?

[6] Kenneth Clarke is a long standing attendee at Bilderberg and, the author believes, a member of the Steering Committee. Perusal of the membership lists of Bilderberg attendees, it is unsurprising how many have been or are involved with European integration (see Pt.II, Chapter.8, Bilderberg).and moves towards further world federalism - TTIP for instance.

Wilson said the same thing during the 1975 Referendum campaign. Both Prime Ministers pretended we had merely joined a Common Market. I fear Margaret Thatcher was deceived as to the way the Single European Act of 1986 would be used, which created the system of Qualified Majority Voting. She bitterly regrets it today[1], as I expect you know. John Major then misled us about the Maastricht Treaty of 1992, and Tony Blair misled us over the Amsterdam Treaty of 1997 and the Nice Treaty of 2002. It has always been essential to keep the true nature of the Project from the British people. They have to be slowly sucked into the embrace of the corrupt octopus, until it is too late to escape.

That is the very essence of the Project, and I hope you will agree it is working pretty well.

---

[1] October 2004.

CHAPTER 7

World Economic Forum (Davos) Strategic Partners (Corporates' Trade Union)[1]

ABB
The Abraaj Group
Accenture
Adecco Group
Adobe Systems Incorporated
Aetna
Agility
Alcoa
ArcelorMittal
AUDI AG

·

Bahrain Economic Development Board
Bain & Company
Bank of America
Barclays
Basic Element
Bill & Melinda Gates Foundation**
Bombardier
Booz & Company
The Boston Consulting Group
BP Plc
Bridgewater Associates
BT
Burda Media

·

CA Technologies
Chevron
Cisco
Citi

---

[1] List taken from World Economic Forum web-site

Clayton, Dubilier & Rice LLC
Clifford Chance
The Coca-Cola Company
Credit Suisse

.

Dalian Wanda Group
Deloitte
Deutsche Bank
Deutsche Post DHL
Dogus Group
The Dow Chemical Company
DuPont

.

Eskom Holdings SOC Limited
EY

.

Fluor Corporation

.

GE
Goldman Sachs
Google Inc.

.

Hanwha Group
HCL Technologies Ltd
Heidrick & Struggles
Henkel
HSBC
Huawei Technologies

.

IHS
Infosys
Intel Corporation
Itaú Unibanco

Jones Lang LaSalle
JPMorgan Chase & Co.
KPMG International
Kudelski Group

.

Lazard
Leighton Holdings Ltd
Lenovo
LIXIL Group Corporation
LUKOIL

ManpowerGroup
Marsh & McLennan Companies (MMC)
McKinsey & Company
METALLOINVEST
Microsoft Corporation
Mitsubishi Corporation
Morgan Stanley

National Bank of Kuwait
Nestlé SA
Novartis
NYSE Euronext

.

The Olayan Group
Old Mutual
Omnicom Group

.

PepsiCo
Petroleo Brasileiro SA - Petrobras
Prudential
Publicis Groupe
PwC

.

Qualcomm

.

Reliance Industries
Renault-Nissan Alliance
The Rockefeller Foundation**
Roland Berger Strategy Consultants
Royal Philips

.

SABMiller
salesforce.com *
Saudi Aramco
Saudi Basic Industries Corporation (SABIC)
Sberbank
Siemens
SK Group
SOCAR (State Oil Company of the Azerbaijan Republic)
Standard Chartered
Swiss International Air Lines
Swiss Re
System Capital Management

Takeda Pharmaceutical
Tata Consultancy Services
Tech Mahindra
Thomson Reuters
Toshiba Corporation

UBS
Unilever

.

VimpelCom
Visa Inc.
Volkswagen AG
VTB Bank

Wipro
WPP

.

Yahoo! Inc.

Zurich Insurance Group

.

*: Strategic Technology Partner
**: Strategic Foundation Partner

CHAPTER 8

Bilderberg

It was only until recently that to talk of Bilderberg was to be labelled a conspiracy theorist and risk losing credibility.

That that remained the situation for decades, is perhaps the measure of their success in keeping their meetings secret. David Rockefeller showed us how it was done when he thanked the media at the 1991 Bilderberg meeting in Baden Baden, Germany (a meeting attended, incidentally, by then-Governor Bill Clinton):

"We are grateful to The Washington Post, The New York Times, Time Magazine, and other great publications whose directors have attended our meetings and respected their promises of discretion for almost forty years. It would have been impossible for us to develop our plan for the world if we had been subject to the lights of publicity during those years. But, the world is now more sophisticated and prepared to march towards a world government. The supranational sovereignty of an intellectual elite[1] and world bankers is surely preferable to the national auto-determination [read 'democracy'] practiced in past centuries."

Thankfully this has changed and the existence of Bilderberg is now an established fact due to the investigative work of a number of campaigners and researchers; even the press now occasionally mention the annual Bilderberg conferences held around the world and questions are sometimes raised in the House of Commons.

For the 2013 conference held at the Grove Hotel, Watford in response to popular indignation, the 'authorities' even provided, together with heavy policing, a few acres for a 'fringe' event where protesters could vent their feeling and listen to speeches (one particularly notable by MP, Michael Meacher)[2].

---

[1] Sounds not unlike 19th century banker Walter Bagehot, author of 'The English Constitution'.

[2] Impromptu interview on various matters including the Constitution given by this writer at the Bilderberg 'fringe' at Watford in 2013 was removed from the internet some 15 months later marked 'CENSORED'.

It's a sobering thought for those of us whose formative years lay in the 1950s, that whilst we were learning of the history of English liberties and democracy and its spread to the then British Empire and commonwealth, that there were those who were plotting in secret to bring those ancient freedoms to an end.

It is true that universal suffrage only had its beginnings in the early 19th century with the Great Reform Act of 1832, but the concept of English liberties had ancient and deep roots stretching back to Anglo Saxon times. The extension of democracy through the vote had not come about as a gift from the ruling aristocracy, but by campaigning and confrontation and from time to time the spilling of blood by the 'lower orders' whose lives were often hard and brutal and where severe punishments were often meted out for the most trivial of offences.

What goes on at Bilderberg

Much has been written about this secret shadowy group, some of it speculative, some of it inaccurate and much of it fanciful. This is hardly surprising, since rumour and speculation is the reverse side of the coin marked secrecy.

For instance critics of Bilderberg have written that the secret group:

— perceives itself as being a supra-governmental;

— manipulates global finances and establishes rigid and binding monetary rates around the world;

— selects political figures whom the Bilderberg decrees should become rulers, and targets those whom it wants removed from power;

— decides which countries shall wage war on others.

But we do get occasional glimpses of what Bilderberg is really about:

Denis Healey, former politician from Britain's Labour Party and early steering committee member, told British journalist Jon

Ronson:

"They don't set policies for the world, they just discuss what the policies should be with the people who can make them happen."

and:

The 1955 Bilderberg summary report, leaked online, notes the:

'Pressing need to bring the German people, together with the other peoples of Europe, into a common market.' and *'To arrive in the shortest possible time at the highest degree of integration, beginning with a common European market.'*

And then we have the testimony of George Crews McGhee, oilman, Rhodes Scholar[3], Ambassador to the Federal Republic of West Germany (1963-68) and Bilderberger attendee (1955-1967), in his book: 'At the Creation of a New Germany: From Adenauer to Brandt: An Ambassador's Account" (1989)':

'The Treaty of Rome which brought the Common Market into being, was nutured at the Bilderberg meetings.'

When asked for an example of a Bilderberg accomplishment George McGhee replied:

'I believe you could say the Treaty of Rome, which brought the Common Market into being, was nurtured at these meetings and aided by the main stream of our discussions there. Prince Bernhard is a great catalyst.'

When Retinger died in 1960, Prince Bernhard paid this tribute to his work:

' .... I am convinced that each and all of us will remember a great man who servd the cause of European unity, Atlantic co-operation and thus World Peace as few others have succeeded in doing.'

And in a letter to the Times 13th June,1960 from Lord Boothby (standing by the windows in the photograph of the 1st Bilderberg meeting in 1954 – this Chapter):

'May I add a few words to Sir Edward Beddington-Behrems's [sic] *admirable*

---

[3] McGhee then spent 3 years at Queen College, Oxford, gaining a doctorate in physical sciences.

tribute to Joseph Retinger?

When a European Confederation comes into existence, as most assuredly it will, it will owe much to his pioneering work. Ever loyal to Poland, to Sikorski, and to his friends, of whom I am proud to have been one, his final loyalty was to the conception of a United Europe: and to this he devoted all his energies and time for the last 15 years.'

Berhens himself in his tribute wrote:

'........ It was he who who inspired the creation of the European Movement which brought about the Council of Europe. The whole development of the idea of the unity of Europe, the creation of the Common Market .... Apart from the European Movement whose aims are largely propagandist and political, it was he who created the European League for Economic Cooperation (ELEC) .... He later founded the Bildeberg Group ...... The meetings, held without any kind of publicity ..... I remember in the United States his picking up the telephone and immediately making an appointment with the President [Eisenhower].'

So who is right – just a talking shop (Healey) or a tool for giant corporations and bankers (who, today, virtually dictate the EU's agenda) – you decide. But essentially the public had been kept in the dark regarding Bilderberg's existence, its raison d'être and its activities. Its existence only came to public attention in 1975 when it was revealed to press that its president since the group's inception in 1954, Prince Bernhard, had accepted illegal backhanders in what became know as the the Lockheed Scandal.

But according to Pierre and Daniel de Villemarest's book, it was a deliberate set-up to get rid of him because David Rockefeller and Henry Kissinger deplored his supposed lack of drive[4]. Jean Monnet, who never participated in Bilderberg meetings, had been complaining that European affairs (meaning European integration) were at a virtual standstill. It was certainly true that during the second half of the 1970s nothing much happened on the federalist

---

4 Facts & Chronicles Denied to the Publice Volume.2: The Secrets of Bilderberg by Pierre & Danielle Villemarest. English translation 2004.

front and if the Villemarests are right about the true reason for getting rid of Prince Bernhard, then his removal is indicative of Bilderberg being more than a talking shop and perhaps a driving force behind integration.

Prince Bernhardt had been a protégé of Joseph Retinger who had selected him because he had been described in a CIA note, dated 30th March 1945, sent by an aide of Allen Dulles, as 'an ambitious man, very easily swayed, unable to choose colleagues wisely' and smitten by society life. Retinger marked him out as being malleable. He was also vulnerable to pressure because of his past with IG-Farben and for his previous Nazi German SS associations.

Claimed Purpose of Bilderberg

Joseph Retinger, founder of Bilderberg, wrote a paper following the May 1956 meeting at Fredensborg, Denmark, in which he described the origins of his creation:

'*A few years ago a large number of people began to feel anxious about a growing distrust of America which was making itself manifest in Western Europe and which was paralleled by a similar distrust of Western Europe in America. This feeling caused considerable apprehension on both sides of the Atlantic and in 1952 I felt that it was of the first importance to try to remove this suspicion, distrust, and lack of confidence which threatened to jeopardize the post-war work of the Western Allies.*'

He then described how he gathered his 'team' together:

'*I ..... approached H.R.H.Prince Bernhard, Dr Paul Rykens, and M. Paul van Zeeland[5] with the suggestion that we should organize some unofficial and private meetings ..... To these meetings we would invite influential and reliable people who carried the respect of those working in the field of national and international affairs and whose personal contact with men at the summit of public activity could help to smooth over these difficulties.*'

[5] Prime Minister of Belguim 1935-37.1939. Van Zeeland became president of the Committee on Refugees, established in London, during the war. In 1946, he was one of the founders of the European League for Economic Cooperation (ELEC). Refer also to the Preface of this book for more on Van Zeeland's activities whilst in London during the War.

Retinger continued: that on the advice of his 'three friends', he approached:

Mr. Hugh Gaitskell, Major-General Sir Colin Gubbins, Mr. Ole Bjorn Kraft, M. Guy Mollet, Dr Rudolf Mueller, M. Antoine Pinay, M. P. Pipinelis, M. Max Brauer, Marshal of the R.A.F. Lord Portal of Hungerford[6], Ambassador Quaroni, and Signor de Gasperi.

The first meeting of this 'pioneering' group took place by, at least, 1956 (date of his paper), the original members (excepting de Gasperi, who had died and been replaced by Signor Amintore Fanfani) were joined by: Sir Terence Airey, Mr. Jens Christian Hauge, Mr. D. Healey, Mr. E. N. van Kleffens, Mr. Reginald Maudling, Mr. Alfred Robens, Professor Carlo Schmid[7], and Mr. Otto Wolff von Amerongen. On the American side there were five members in addition to Mr. Johnson, viz.: Mr. George Ball, Mr. John H. Ferguson, Mr. H. J. Heinz, Mr. George Nebolsine, and Mr. Dean Rusk.

These men, there were no women, together formed Retinger's Steering Committee, an arrangement which continues to the present day. It is the Steering Committee that sets the agenda based upon the objectives of Bilderberg set out by Retinger in the first place. It also decides whom to invite to their annual meetings.

The Steering Committee meets from time to time and *'Subjects which do not need a long preparation as far as papers to be presented are concerned, and for which an attendance of fifteen to twenty people seems sufficient, are discussed from time to time in this smaller group'.*

Retinger reported that up to the time of his paper, *'The themes discussed were'*:

The attitude towards Communism and the Soviet Union.

The attitude towards dependent areas and peoples overseas.

The attitude towards economic policies and problems.

---

[6] The author recalls Lord Portal, a 'gun', whilst working as a beater on Saturdays at shoots in the Savernake Forest near Marlborough.

[7] In 1940 he was made legal counsel of the 'Oberfeldkommandantur' of the German occupation forces in Lille (France).

The attitude towards European integration and the European Defence Community.

Communist infiltration in various Western countries.

The Uncommitted Peoples:

(a) political and ideological aspects;
(b) economic aspects.

Article 2 of the North Atlantic Treaty:

The political and strategic aspects of atomic energy.

The reunification of Germany.

European unity.

The industrial aspects of atomic energy.

Economic problems:

(a) East-West trade.

(b) The political aspects of convertibility.

(c) Expansion of international trade.

The causes of the growth of anti-Western blocs, in particular in the United Nations.

The role played by anti-colonialism in the relations between Asians and Westerners.

A common approach by the Western world towards China and the emergent nations of South and East Asia.

The Communist campaign for political subversion or control of the newly emancipated countries of Asia.

Retinger then continued by describing the qualities of those to be invited to annual Bilderberg conferences:

'*The first essential is undoubtedly to have men of absolute personal and political integrity; the second, to have men of real international standing, or whose position in their own countries is such as to give them considerable influence in at least an important section of the population, men who in their own field hold a position of authority and enjoy the confidence of their fellow-men;*'

Note the international, elitist flavour, of those deemed suitable for Bilderberg meetings. In fact this 'club' was to specifically exclude any with attachment to nation-state with Retinger's third requirement:

'the third, to have men with no obvious nationalistic bias ......'

This 'club' had its genesis on 25th September 1952, at 18 rue de l'Assumption, Paris, 16th arrondissement, which began at 10am, with most of the 12 initiates, including the British leader of the Labour opposition, Hugh Gaitskell, present.

Records show that this meeting had been some time in preparation with papers prepared for the meeting as early as July 1952 by Guy Mollet and Marshall of the Royal Airforce, Lord Portal of Hungerford.

The first full Bilderberg conference (the group only later came to call themselves Bilderberg – after the hotel in the little town of Oosterbeek, Holland where they met) was a four day affair held from 28th to 31th May 1954.

The venue chosen had a curious association with WWII. It was at Oosterbeek that the British 1st Airborne Division had been dropped almost 10 years previously, on Sunday, 17th September 1944, into the area as part of operation 'Market Garden' designed to end the war by Christmas that year. It resulted in a tragic defeat for the lightly armed paratroopers who encountered two panzer divisions 'refitting' in the area.

The area around Hotel Bilderberg, named Hotel Tafelberg at the time of the battle, was the scene of fierce fighting, when the 3rd Parachute Battalion encountered a well dug in Battalion Krafft blocking progress to Arnhem Bridge. This was a fatal set-back, as only one of three designated battalions[8] was able to make it through

---

[8] 1st Battalion under Col. Frost. The story can be heard on CD (available from the author) and can also be accessed on U-tube: http://www.youtube.com/watch?v=50ogHjrQFBE . It lasts one hour and the stories of major participants in the battle can be heard – notably that of Captain Moffatt Burriss who led a company of the American 504th Parachute Regiment across the Waal River at Nijmegan in a spirited and dangerous attempt to relieve the British 1st Parachute Battalion defending the bridge at Arnhem. The story of Brigade Major Tony Hibbert who took over the defence after Col. Frost was seriously wounded, complements that of Moffatt Burris.

and effectively meant the failure of Market Garden to achieve its chief objective.

One wonders whether the British delegation that May was aware of the significance of the choice of venue for their first historic meeting, and if they had, whether they cared. Certainly delegate Major General Gubbins, wartime head of SOE, should have been.

Retinger's Bilderberg initiative was, in retrospect, clearly part of a grand plan for global governance through the abolition of nation states, so loathed by global corporatists and international bankers. There could be no place in the grand scheme of things for democracy and social justice.

Retinger, in 1952, was embarking upon his second historic secret global project – to unite men (or their agents) of influence and power together, a project that would continue to the present day.

The grip that Bilderberger and similar parallel international organisations have on power today trumps national democracy and reduces the power of individuals to ashes. Power should spring from the people, but the activities of people like Joseph Retinger, have ensured that this is but a fading dream.

Retinger's first major triumph of course had been to draw the USA, through ACUE[9], into financing and supporting the failing European Movement in 1948.

Retinger's European Movement had been an essential ingredient for the elites to kick-start the European Union (without the EM, there would have been no EU) project as has been well documented elsewhere in this book. It was the supposed common people demanding European integration, when in fact they had no such interest.

The reality was that the European Movement was paid for, and owned by global corporatists and international bankers. Bilderberg is and was secret power elites plotting together for the demise of nation states through massive media propaganda, the interference in the democratic process and their involvement in the selection

---

[9] American Committee for a United Europe, see Pt.II, Chapter.1 of this book.

and sometimes 'de-selection' of national leaders.

Joseph Retinger – a profile

Retinger, a Fabian and close friend of Joseph Conrad was born in 1888 in Kraków in what is now Poland. He studied political science gaining a PhD from the Sorbonne in 1908.

Retinger was a close friend of the Polish General Wladyslaw Sikorski who led free Polish forces in Britain during the Second World War. He parachuted into Poland[10] in 1944 at the age of 56, possibly in connection with the Salamandar Affair[11].

On 4th July 1943, General Sikorski was killed in an aircraft crash when his plane was taking off from Gibraltar for London – he had been visiting Polish General Anders in the Middle East. For the first time Sikorski had to fly without his aide, Joseph Retinger. Retinger had told Sikorski he would not be accompanying him – it was the first time Sikorski had flown on a trip without his Aide. The Czeck pilot, Eduard Prchal, was the only survivor and came under suspicion because when he was rescued from the sea he was wearing his life-jacket – normally he flew without one[12].

Retinger, besides Bilderberg[13], founded the European League for Economic Cooperation (ELEC) together with Paul Van Zeeland (Belgium), and Pieter Kerstens (Holland) in 1946. They were soon joined by Edmond Giscard d'Estaing (France), Harold Butler (United Kingdom) and Hermann Joseph Abs[14] (Germany).

---

10 According to Pierre & Danielle Villemarest (see footnote earlier in this Chapter).

11 Implied by Pierre & Danielle Villemarest.

12 Pierre & Danielle Villemarest claim Sikorski was assassinated and Retinger, by implication, gets the blamed.

13 As we saw earlier, Retinger also saved the European Movement from collapse with financial aid from ACUE.

14 Herman Abs known as Hitler's banker was responsible for financing the German war effort and was a friend of Martin Borman. Banker Baron Kurt von Schroeder commented that "Abs was particularly important to the Third Reich". Abs arranged the financing of Auschwitz slave labour concentration camp (set up to produce synthetic rubber and fuel). After the war Abs narrowly missed prosecution at Nuremberg helped by influential friends in the USA and Britain and went on to lobby for the release of imprisoned industrialists. After the war Abs retained his position of Chairman of Deutsche Bank and director of I.G Farben (subsequently broken up and renamed) as well as several other important positions, including directing the spending of

The League led directly to the formation of today's European Union.

Retinger died in London in 1960.

Hugh Gaitskell - Prime Minister in waiting

Hugh Gaitskell became leader of the Labour Party Opposition in 1955 following the retirement of Clement Attlee.

Gaitskell was regarded highly, and many expected him to become a great prime minister. But following his untimely death he became known to Labour supporters as the 'best prime minister we never had'.

It was clear that Joseph Retinger regarded him in the same way, which no doubt, was the reason he was invited to participate in the inaugural meeting of, what came to be known as Bilderberg, in Paris on 25th September 1952. Retinger would already have spotted him as a future prime minister and sought to have him as part of the federalist group.

At first Gaitskell was an enthusiastic contributing member of Bilderberg and its Steering Group. He can be seen in the photograph included in this Chapter, seated in the far right hand corner in deep contemplation next to a smoking General Gubbins

Hugh Gaitskell

at the first full meeting held in the Bilderberg Hotel, Oosterbeek, Holland from 28th to 31th May 1954.

But as time went on it was clear that Gaitskell was becoming more detached from the Group, sending apologies to invitations to Bilderberg meetings for being unable to attend.

American Marshal Aid. Abs became a member of the European Movement Finance Sub-Committee and in August 1949 became a member of the German Council of the European Movement. All in all, Abs was a very successful and very busy man with fingers in many pies.

This was in line with the increasing detachment of British politicians from federalist organizations until the shock of Suez. The British and French Suez intervention was triggered by the withdrawal of American aid to Egypt for their Aswan Dam project and the subsequent nationalization of the canal by President Gamel Abdel Nasser.

Gaitskell, who many expected to become prime minister after the election due by 1964, made a long impassioned and reasoned speech at the Labour Party annual conference in Brighton on the 3rd October 1962. The part dealing with the EEC is worth repeating here:

'We must be clear about this: it does mean, if this is the idea, the end of Britain as an independent European state. I make no apology for repeating it. It means the end of a thousand years of history. You may say 'Let it end' but, my goodness, it is a decision that needs a little care and thought. And it does mean the end of the Commonwealth. How can one really seriously suppose that if the mother country, the centre of the Commonwealth, is a province of Europe (which is what federation means) it could continue to exist as the mother country of a series of independent nations? It is sheer nonsense.'

Gaitskell then turned to the question of who should take the decision to join, alluding to the prickly subject of a referendum:

Of course, Mr. Macmillan has given a pledge in his broadcast. He said: 'When we know the final position, then it will be for us here in Britain to decide what to do.' For us here in Britain? Who does he mean? Does he mean the Government? Or the Tory Party? Or the British people? We are now being told that the British people are not capable of judging this issue — the Government know best; the top people are the only people who can understand it; it is too difficult for the rest. This is the classic argument of every tyranny in history. It begins as a refined, intellectual argument, and it moves into a one-man dictatorship; 'We know best' becomes 'I know best.' We did not win the political battles of the 19th and 20th centuries to have this reactionary nonsense thrust upon us again.

So the leader of the Opposition and Prime Minister in waiting had turned his and the Party's back on the EEC. Then three months later, quite unexpectedly, he was dead. He died in 18th January 1963, aged 56, from, as given[15] in the post mortem examination report, lupus erythematosus, an autoimmune disease.

'He entered Manor House Hospital on 15th December complaining of pains in his arms and legs and across his shoulders. His medical history contained in the postmortem shows that his only previous ailment was a chest pain in 1945[16].'

Gaitskell had previously, in the Autumn of 1962, planned a trip to Moscow at the invitation of Soviet leader Nikita Khrushchev. Gaitskell never got there having died.

Foul play was suspected and Porton Down's disease specialist Dr. Ladell considered it as a possible murder – 'nothing to prove it', was the verdict.

There are some stories as to how he might have been 'poisoned' at the hands of the Soviets, the most credible being that it happened when he visited the Soviet Embassy in London on 13th December and consumed the tea and crumpets provided[17]. It would have been expected of course that he would have visited the Embassy preparatory to his planned visit to Moscow, but far fetched to speculate that he was fatally poisoned there.

The whole theory that the Soviets murdered Gaitskell is fanciful, it was a story encouraged by Peter Wright in his book 'Spycatcher', which in turn was inspired by Anatoliy Golitsyn, the Soviet KGB defector and James Jesus Angleton, Chief of the CIA's Counter-intelligence staff from 1954 to 1975.

Robin Ramsay, investigative journalist of Lobster Magazine, has told me that he doesn't believe Gaitskell was murdered. But if he

---

[15] This writer has not seen the Report, but there is sufficient written about it in the public domain to suppose it to be true.

[16] 'The Age', Tuesday, 31st March 1981.

[17] 'The Wedge: The Secret war between the FBI and CIA, by Mark Riebling, Simon and Scuster, June 2010.

is wrong, and this writer doesn't think so, then had not American interests[18] as much as Soviet, a motive for removing Gaitskell?[19]. And would the Soviet Union be so blatant in its methods?

Whatever the cause of Gaitskell's death, what is certain is that democracy and national sovereignty were the losers and corporatism, if it had tears, did not shed them.

Harold Wilson became the new Party leader and narrowly won the next general election for Labour 21 months later. He went on to make a second application for Britain to join the EEC. That he failed might indicate that he may not have been too serious in his quest[20].

First full meeting of Bilderbrg – Oosterbeek 28th-31st May 1954

---

[18] Federalising Europe and removal of obstacles to achieving that goal.

[19] Replacing Hugh Gaitskell with Harold Wilson (who went on to become Prime Minister) happened because, as the Wright conspiracy theories goes, 'he was their man'.

[20] Tony Benn attended a Referendum Movement meeting in the early 2000s to speak; he told me: 'Y'know – Wilson never really wanted to join the Common Market'. At the time this writer didn't believe him, but a dozen years later he does. For those wishing to know more, it's worth reading Robin Ramsay's 1996 article in Lobster Journal, issue.cc, ISSN: 0964-0436.

Joseph Retinger - Bilderberg founder

"DE BILDERBERG" CONFERENCE

at Oosterbeek

29th, 30th, 31st May 1954

PRESIDENT: His Royal Highness, The Prince of the Netherlands.

VICE-PRESIDENTS: Coleman, John S.
van Zeeland, Paul.

SECRETARY GENERAL: Retinger, J.H.

RAPPORTEURS: Ball, George W.   U.S.A.
Lawyer.

     Bingham, George Barry   U.S.A.
Newspaper publisher.
Chief of Mission to France.
Economic Cooperation Administration,
1949-1950.

     Gaitskell, The Rt. Hon. H.T.N.

     U.K.
Member of Parliament.
Former Chancellor of the Exchequer.

     De Gasperi, Alcide   Italy.
Member of Parliament.
Former Prime Minister.

     Hirschfeld, H.M.   Netherlands.
Economic Adviser to the Netherlands'
Government.
Former High Commissioner of the
Netherlands' Government in
Indonesia.
Director of Companies.

     Mollet, Guy   France.
Member of Parliament.
Former Deputy Prime Minister.
Secretary General of the Socialist
Party.

     Nitze, Paul H.   U.S.A.
President, Foreign Service
Educational Foundation.
Director, Policy Planning Staff,
Dept. of State, 1950-1953.

     de la Vallée Poussin, Etienne

     Belgium.
Senator.

Rockefeller, David   U.S.A.
Banker
Senior Vice-President, The Chase
National Bank.

Zellerbach, J.D.   U.S.A.
Industrialist.
Member U.S. Delegation, General
Assembly of United Nations, 1953.
Chief, ECA Special Mission to
Italy, 1948-1950.

x   x
x

André, Robert   France.
President of the "Syndicat du
Pétrole".

Assheton, The Rt. Hon Ralph
U.K.
Member of Parliament.
Former Parliamentary Secretary to
Ministry of Supply, Former Financial
Secretary to the Treasury.

de Beaumont, G.   France.
Member of Parliament.

Bonvoisin, Pierre   Belgium.
Banker.
President of the "Banque de la
Société Générale de Belgique".

Boothby, Sir Robert   U.K.
Member of Parliament.

Brauer, Max   Germany.
Former Mayor and President of the
Land of Hamburg.

Cafiero, Raffaele   Italy.
Senator.

Cisler, Walker L.   U.S.A.
Public Utility Executive.
President, The Detroit Edison Co.
Consultant to Atomic Energy
Commission and Mutual Security
Agency.

Cowles, Gardner   U.S.A.
Publisher.

Davies, The Rt. Hon. Clement
U.K.
Member of Parliament.
Former Minister.
Chairman of Parliamentary Liberal
Party.

-3-

Drapier, Jean	Belgium. Lawyer.
Duchet, R.	France. Member of Parliament. Former Minister, Secretary General Independants and Peasants Party.
Faure, M.	France. Member of Parliament.
Ferguson, John H.	U.S.A. Lawyer. Vice-President and Executive Direc Director, Cttee. for a National Trade Policy. Deputy Director, Policy Planning Staff, Dept. of State, 1951-1953.
Foster, John	U.K. Member of Parliament. Parliamentary Under-Secretary of State for Commonwealth Relations.
Franks, The Rt. Hon. Sir Oliver	U.K. Former Ambassador in Washington. Chairman Lloyd's Bank.
Geyer, Gerhard P.Th.	Germany. Industrialist. Director General "Esso".
Gubbins, Sir Colin	U.K. Major General retd. Formerly in charge of SOE.
Healey, Denis W.	U.K. Member of Parliament. Former Secretary of the International Cttee. of the Labour Party.
Heinz, H.J.	U.S.A. Industrialist. President H.J. Heinz Co.
Høegh, Leif	Norway. Shipowner.
Jackson, C.D.	U.S.A. Publisher. Formerly Special Assistant to President Eisenhower 1953-1954.
Jay, Nelson Dean	U.S.A. Banker. Director, J.P. Morgan & Co. Inc. New York.

-4-

Kanellopoulos, P.	Greece. Member of Parliament. Minister of National Defence.
Koningsberger, V.J.	Netherlands. Professor State University Utrecht.
Kraft, Ole Bjørn	Denmark. Member of Parliament. Former Foreign Minister.
Leverkuehn, P.M.A.	Germany. Lawyer. Member of Parliament.
Malagodi, Giovanni F.	Italy. Member of Parliament.
Moe, Finn	Norway. Member of Parliament. Chairman, Parliamentary Foreign Affairs Cttee. Vice-President, Council of Europe.
Montgomery Hyde, H.	U.K. Member of Parliament.
Motz, Roger	Belgium. Senator. Chairman of the Liberal International Former Chairman of the Liberal Party.
Mueller, Rudolf	Germany. Lawyer.
McGhee, George C.	U.S.A. Industrialist. Assistant Secretary of State for Near Eastern & South African Affairs, 1949-1952. U.S. Ambassador and Chief, American Mission for Aid to Turkey, 1951-1953.
Nebolsine, George	U.S.A. Lawyer. Consultant to Department of State and Economic Cooperation Administration 1948, Trustee U.S. Council of International Chamber of Commerce.
Oosterhuis, H.	Netherlands. Member of Parliament. President of the Netherlands Federation of Trade Unions.

Parker, Cola G.	U.S.A. Industrialist. Member of Commission on Foreign Economic Policy (Randall Commission).
Perkins, George W.	U.S.A. Industrialist. Assistant Secr. of State for European Affairs, 1949-1953.
Pilkington, Sir Harry	U.K. President, Federation of British Industries.
Pinay, Antoine	France. Member of Parliament. Former Prime Minister.
Pipinelis, P.	Greece. Former Foreign Minister. Former Ambassador to U.S.S.R.
Pirelli, Alberto	Italy. Industrialist. Minister of State.
Quaroni, P.	Italy. Ambassador to France. Former Ambassador to the U.S.S.R.
Rosenberg, Ludwig	Germany. Chief of Department of Foreign Affairs of the Trade Unions.
Rossi, Paolo	Italy. Member of Parliament.
De Rougemont, Denis	Switzerland. Author. Director European Cultural Centre.
Rijkens, Paul	Netherlands. Industrialist. Chairman of Unilever N.V.
Schneider, Ernst Georg	Germany. Industrialist. President, Chamber of Commerce of Düsseldorf.
Spang, Joseph P. Jr.	U.S.A. Industrialist. President, The Gillette Co.
Steenberghe, M.P.L.	Netherlands. Former Minister of Economic Affairs of the Netherlands. Director of Companies.

Teitgen, P.H.	France. Vice President of the Council of Ministers.
Terkelsen, Terkel M.	Denmark. Chief Editor, Berlingske Tidende.
Tingsten, Herbert L.G.	Sweden. Chief Editor, Dagens Nyheter.
Troeger, H.	Germany. Minister of Finance of Hesse.
Valletta, Vittorio	Italy. Industrialist. President of Fiat.
Voisin, André	France. President "La Fédération".
Waldenström, M.	Sweden. Industrialist.
van Walsem, H.F.	Netherlands. Industrialist. Member of the Board of Philips Industries Eindhoven.
Willems, Jean	Belgium. "Fondation Universitaire".
Williamson, Tom	U.K. General Secretary, National Union of General and Municipal Workers.

x   x

x

IN AN ADVISORY CAPACITY:

Vlekke, B.H.M.	Netherlands. Secretary General of the Netherlands Society of International Affairs.

SECRETARIAT:	Director:	Veenstra, W.
	Secretaries:	Canali, E.
		Focke, E.G.
		Littlejohn, E.
		Overweg, G.E.
		Pomian, J.

155

CHAPTER 9

Profile of a pro-European
(although not untypical, the character described here is purely fictitious)

A few years ago I suggested to Tommy we might meet for lunch, just for the hell of it really; agreeing, we met up in a poshish Cotswold Hotel on a cold, icy, January day.

The notion had come to me after several years of almost mutual hostility, I, a committed anti-European, and Tommy the opposite, a committed pro-European working for the European Movement. Of course I'm not in any way anti-European but decided to play the game of pejoratives – just to please him. Of course those of us opposed to the European Union do so on grounds of democracy, sovereignty and a few other isms thrown in. I think Tommy understands that, but argues the EU is all of those things – well he has to.

I don't know Tommy's motives for meeting me, but myself, I wanted to get inside his brain to understand what it was that made him such a corporatist.

He must have thought me stupid as he began with a lecture to convince me of the merits of the EU. I stopped him dead and said that there was no point in this as he was no more likely to convince me, as I him.

He recognised what I proposed was sensible in the situation and our discussion took a different, more interesting course, prompted by my asking about his career, which I knew had been as an officer in the Guards and that he had at one time been wounded in action. I had understood that, that was fighting in Korea in the early 1950s, but was wrong, he had been wounded in action in Tanganyika quelling natives. In his own words he was leading his platoon and the bloke behind had 'accidentally' loosed his rifle, which had hit him in the arm, causing a non-disabling injury.

Tommy in fact had been born on the North West Frontier, a fractious place at any time, but especially so when ruled by the white men. His father, he told me, was some sort of Raj official who, on retirement (these sort of people retired quite early in those days) from the Service, moved to Australia.

Young Tommy had, in the line of duty expected of him, joined the Australian Army, but thought better of it, transferring to the British Army (not sure whether as an officer, I forgot to ask him). He joined a Guards' Regiment and was certainly a subaltern by the time his Regiment was posted to Tanganyika.

He left the army soon afterwards as he realised that pay and conditions were unsuitable to his newly married status and got into the second-hand car market and scrap steel, although he didn't call it that. Tommy was fond of proclaiming to anyone who would listen that he 'got into old bangers and steel', steel was the future.

Whenever Tommy spoke publicly, which was often, he rattled on about how we must be in the EU to obtain the economies of scale etc to compete with China.

Tommy of course was fed from a young age tales of the British Empire, daring do, and all it's glory. It was Tanganyika and retreat from Empire, which fired up Tommy, and no doubt his father too.

This was no time for Empire builders in the traditional sense, the last gasp having taken place at Suez in 1956, the Empire was dying on its feet. What was needed was an ending of the old rivalry between European nations fighting over colonial spoils and a 'pooling of sovereignty'[1] so that a new Empire might emerge. It was supposed to be a bigger and more successful empire because the drivers – were 'Europe United'. This was not just Tommy talking, we heard it from Geoffrey Tucker, Heath's campaigning guru in the early 1970s and we heard it from the leader of the pro-Euro Conservative Party, John Stevens, until his Party was

---

[1] The battle cry employed to try and persuade public opinion that the whole was greater than the sum of the parts, not realising the bigger the pool the smaller the fish, relatively speaking, in it.

wound up with just one percent of the vote in the 1999 European Parliament elections. We heard this kind of talk again recently from the Prime Minister, David Cameron, with his vision of a 'European Union stretching from the Atlantic to the Urals'[2]. What sort of inferiority complex do these people suffer from that they need an empire?

This 'group-think, mind-set' came from humiliation and defeat before and after Suez in 1956, the latter being the determinant. It was then that mandarins and colonial administrators got wind up, panicked and looked to similar windy megalomaniacs across the Channel. It is unsurprising that Brussels and its bureaucratic elite feel so comfortable in their new ivory tower pulling the levers of power[3].

During lunch Tommy got carried away a bit talking about those he was chasing around East Africa, referred to them sometimes in the most unmentionable of terms.

To give Tommy his due, when getting him to expand on the empire theme, he denied that he was really looking for a white European substitute empire. But he would say that wouldn't he?

Tommy later sent me a thoughtful email making a few claims and observations, which may help further in evaluating the profile of a pro-European:

1. The EU is the first ever voluntary union of democratic nation states where no one is forced to join and anyone can leave if that is the the wish of the democratically elected government (not the people of course, never the people).

2. Brown [Gordon, Prime Minister] is a tedious man and a tedious speaker but America is a disgraceful nation where, for example, 36 million people live below the poverty line, 47 million have no health cover and a further 40 million have totally inadequate emergency

---

[2] Reported by Christopher Booker, Daily Telegraph, 20th December 2014.

[3] Or the modern keyboard equivalent of levers of power.

only, health cover. The Centre and South, to my personal knowledge, is rampant with racism.

3. America's idea of national sovereignty is that they are allowed to interfere with armed intervention in anyone else's country whenever they wish.

4. The basics of the Christian, Jewish, Muslim, Hindhu, Sikh and Buddhist religions are the same, based on love God and your neighbour. The trouble is that all of them get taken over and distorted by man.

Having spend the best part of 2 hours in Tommy's company, I can see in this email, things I can empathise with, things that are hypocritical and much that is totally untrue – can the reader work out which?

Sadly, Tommy is no longer with us.

Postscript

The Rats

Anyone obstructing the 'Project', one that comes in different stripes: New World Order, Global Governance, European Union or whatever guise corporate dominance shows itself, is liable to attract a measure of invective. This usually comes from those who should know better. Activists, whether amateur or one of the few professional politicians who have a mind of their own will recognise this[1] – look back at 1992 and Prime Minister, John Major's give-away of sovereignty and the public's democratic powers and rights at Maastricht[2].

[signature]

[signature]

Signatories of Maastricht Treaty 1992

The preceding chapters have been replete with officially sponsored trashing of the hard won gains of the previous two centuries (the franchise) and denial of the English (Scotland has its own) written

---

[1] Some will remember Prime Minister, John Major's 'bastards'.
[2] Treaty of Maastricht was signed by Francis Maude and Douglas Hurd (Lord Hurd).

CONFIDENTIAL

<u>Europe: Parliament and Public Opinion</u>

<u>TIMING</u>

1.   It has always been agreed that once the
negotiations got moving towards a successful
outcome both interest and the degree of approval
would increase dramatically. But once the
negotiations are adjourned for the summer there
is bound to be a falling-off in interest and
there will be considerable loss of momentum.

2.   Therefore the Government should exploit
the impetus of this stage of negotiations by
seeking to commit as many people as possible as
far as possible. This will tide us over the
vacuum left by the Summer and stand the Government
in good stead as the final decisions are taken
at the end of the year. The converse is also true:
once the momentum is lost 'the rats' will begin
to get at public, parliamentary and 'informed'
opinion.

<u>An early vote?</u>

3.   All this points to obtaining an approving
vote of some kind in Parliament before the Summer
recess.

4.   The chief objections against such an early
vote are that public opinion will not have had time
to change appreciably, that it would be dangerous
to give the impression of trying to 'bounce' MPs
into taking a decision, and that it would place
pro-European Labour MPs in an intolerable position
to expect them to stand up and be counted so soon
after a negative vote at their special Party Conference
on July 24.

5.   None of these objections seems to outweigh
the disadvantages of losing the initiative which
the new momentum would give the Government.
Nevertheless, each can be met to a large extent.

Rats Memo, 10.05.71: Report covering memo to Prime Minister, Edward Heath
advising on the campaign to gain support of Parliament and Public Opinion.

Constitution and much more[3].

This book's underlying theme has been the corporatists who now largely make this World the way it is. But enough has now been written of this excepting to explain this Chapter's title.

The memo by some high official, (opposite), no doubt empathizing with the Prime Minister, summarizes better than anything else the corporate mind-set towards the rest of us who don't agree with it.

This book in exploring Britain's political history regarding Europe over 50 years or so, has been realistic, if pessimistic, about the human condition. But it would fail without a glance at the future. George Orwell in books like '1984' painted a hopeless future and provided a timely warning when democracy and liberty seemed secure[4]. No critical history would be worth anything without proposals for change. Clearly the larger a political entity becomes, the further removed the elector is from democracy and the possibility of enjoying any influence over the way our's and our family's lives we are governed and taxed.

For instance taxation has become an unnecessary minefield, no one really knows how much of earned money is removed in taxation. At an estimate, based upon adding together all monies ending up in government and local government coffers between 70 and 80% are removed from a middle-class earner[5]. Can we control it - no!

Anyway, I asked friends and colleagues what ought to be done to put things right, to find ways of returning democracy and some

---

[3] This writer has particularly in mind planning laws made at the highest levels which look no further ahead than the ends of noses, where towns march incessantly over landscapes, where no petition or argument makes the slightest bit of difference, where future generations are ignored. The thought of those that gain are, no doubt - we shall not be here to see the result of our 'labours'.

[4] This writer considers Orwell's: '*If you want a vision of the future, think of a boot, stamping on a head, for ever – don't let it happen*'. It is worth contemplating today and there are those working to head this off, but we are already down the road and much more effort by more is needed.

[5] Totalling together such items as: income tax; National Insurance (employees and employers); VAT; vehicle tax; stamp duty on house purchase (big item as workers have to move so much more often that previously seeking work); council tax; loss of value on savings due to inflation and if there's anything left when you die a portion is taxed at 40% (2014) through Death Duties (Inheritance Tax).

control over lives to the public at large.

One friend thought it needed MPs to be more responsive to those who'd elected them. I agreed, but pointed out that politicians these days, at least, owe their position to the party and usually will support the party's position whenever there is conflict between a constituency resident's interests and the party. Understandable of course when it's realised where the main source of governing party's funding comes from. It's called representative government – work that one out.

So what's to be done? Well, if I've got this book and its title right, then the solution is obvious, though of course difficult to realise. Corporate business and banking in particular, has been allowed to grow beyond what is healthy. Over a period of at least 50 years governments have approved merger after merger to the point where governments can only with the greatest of difficulty legislate for them. Large corporations spread themselves globally where they can play one country off against one another and are able to avoid paying anything like their fair share of tax.

The EU is largely corporatist and created by them. These global behemoths not only created the EU, they lobby it and now are working to intensify their global reach through TTIP, the 'Trans Atlantic Trade and Investment Partnership'. The EU and the US Government are presently negotiating a giant free trade agreement which include plans to allow investors[6] to sue whole nations through 'Investor State Dispute Settlement' clauses.

Campaigners are already alert to the dangers, which they claim will impinge on democratic accountability [assuming of course democracy still has life in its body] and pose a threat to public funds and public policy. One can see unlimited threats to nations and therefore ordinary individuals if these corporate powers see the light of day.

---

[6] The cost involved in suing governments would be enormous, so what is planned is not for the benefit of ordinary mortals.

So what's to be done?

In the not too distant past anti-trust legislation would have ensured corporations didn't get too big for their boots and was probably last used in a major way with the break-up of the American Bell telephone monopoly. The break-up was initiated by the US Government in 1974 and completed some 10 years later.

In Britain the 'Monopolies and Mergers Commission', with roots stretching back to 1949, was constituted in 1965 and sought to keep corporations at a manageable size. It became just the 'Competition Commission' in 1999, with, it seems, the arm dealing with mergers abolished[7].

Corporatism has been identified in this book as a, or the, leading problem today, and although trade unionism can be damaging as well, the former has been very much in the ascendency in recent decades with trade unionism bereft of its teeth.

This book makes no crusading claim, but clearly corporatism is a problem and laws to keep the problem in check now seem to be ineffective or no longer exist.

So solution number one is to elect a government with the will and the ability to deal with this issue[8]. That is a government that represents the people not corporatists, so that they will not feel unable to legislate to make the market place work properly again. What this government would then need to do would be to put in place a programme of de-mergers bringing the component parts down to manageable size and make them nation-based again. This would, besides making them more controllable, bring competition back into the system.

In parallel with this, those public utilities that have been handed over to to these giant corporations who it seems pay little tax, will need to be brought back under public ownership. We are talking here about utilities which inherently do not lend themselves to

---

7 Research needed.
8 UKIP seems to have no policies on the matter.

competition – electricity supply (the right to switch suppliers has not worked, being impracticable because suppliers rates are subject to change (upwards of course) and keeping up with the electricity market place is too time consuming for the average householder); water, gas and railways. Privatised postal services are now so costly that few can indulge in the old fashioned habit of letter writing and of course campaigning by post is out of the question – perhaps that's the intention.

The level of compensation for industries brought back under state control would depend upon audited profits made over the years.

However the telecommunications industry is quite suitable for competition and as such would not need to be brought back as a public utility.

The utilities (family silver[9]) taken back under public ownership would of course sometimes need subsidising, but those who object to that should remember that the privatised railways receive heavy subsidies and even then private companies tend to walk away when subsidies were not generating sufficient profit.

This writer would add that if the State is unable to make basic provisions: health care, postal service, then what is the State actually for?

These chapters have also touched on constitutional issues and claimed that constitutions are there to proscribe powers of governments and to protect the public from overweening government. It is worth stating again the Thomas Paine political philosophy (Thomas Paine test say):

"[G]overnment has no right to make itself a party in any debate respecting the principles or modes of forming, or of changing, constitutions. It is not for the benefit of those who exercise the powers of government, that constitutions, and the governments issuing from them, are established."

---

[9] Expression used by former Prime Minister, Harold Macmillan, to describe Margaret Thatcher's privatizations in the 1980s.

Paine added this rider:

"A constitution is the property of a nation, and not of those who exercise government".

However the UK Government wants free rein, ignoring our written Constitution[10], whilst at the time of writing, it is developing its own Bill of Rights. So perhaps the Government should consider this observation by Thomas Paine:

A long habit of not thinking a thing wrong gives it a superficial appearance of being right.

Dealing with corporations and constitutions should go a long way to improving matters, but we should consider briefly the sticky issue of monarchy. Monarchical government has been part of the rich tapestry of British and English life for over a 1000 years; it has worked after a fashion and perhaps it could continue to do so if the Monarchy was given a real role. That governments have been able to ride rough-shod over the written Constitution and strip the Monarchy of power shows that a truly independent guardian, able to protect the people from overweening power, is needed. Perhaps the Monarchy, if equipped with its own office and given power for enforcing observance of the Constitution upon governments, could be that guardian?

Putting corporations back in their box would surely lead to solutions to many ills that have developed under their malign influence. For instance we saw corporatism in 2013, in the guise of secretive Bilderberg,[11] able to call upon hundreds of British police,[12] to surround the Grove Hotel estate outside Watford, for their annual three day conference.

Yet in this writer's experience, as well as those of some of his friends

---

10 The EU also has a Constitution which the British are required to observe, so how all these constitutions fit together is a mystery to this writer, maybe that is the intention.

11 What they were planning for the World was not reported – the media hardly touched on the conference's existence. This extra-democratic gathering received homage by the attendance of the British Prime Minister, David Cameron, another demonstration of corporate power.

12 This was not a football match, an event which normally benefit the public.

and colleagues, often encounter when in need of help, official disinterest at best, or threat of arrest from one of a bunch of potential charges now populating the law book – wasting police time, being one of the most popular. On top of that we now see the State recruiting a new kind of policeman – the thug.

Good policing needs the confidence of the public – the friendly reassuring bobby on the beat, not just boy racers in their flash fast cars, sirens blaring. And intimidating black paramilitary uniforms with weaponry displayed to frighten.

The continent has always been this way, but harmonisation – what a lovely sounding word – didn't come to mean the spread of our benign policing over there, instead it meant, adoption of things European. Well, they say you can never go back, but that does not mean things don't have to be radically re-thought as part of this, 'What's to be done', so that people benefit, not just the few.

Bibliography

'A Letter to the Times', (audio track), available on CD: 'shoe-horned into EU'

A Hard Pounding, Dr Peter Gardner

A political life, Tony Benn

Approach to Europe, 1970/71, National Archive document, FCO 26/1215

Architects of the Cold War, Prof. Paul S. Cutter

At the creation of a new Germany - from Adenauer to Brandt – an ambassador's account, oilman and American Ambassador to Germany, George McGhee

Black Arrow Rocket papers, National Archive records, CAB 164/859

Blowback, Christopher Simpson

Booker Column, Sunday Telegraph, 24th July 2005

Britain Held Hostage, Lindsay Jenkins

Britain's Secret Propaganda War, Paul Lashmar and James Oliver

Coronation Oath

Declaration and Bill of Rights (1689),

Disappearing Britain, Lindsay Jenkins

European Communities Act 1972 (ECA72)

Evan's Euro Adventure, 30th March, 2003, Evan Davis, BBC Economic Editor

Facts & Chronicles Denied to the Public, Volume.2: The secrets of Bilderberg, Pierre & Danielle Villemarest – English translation, 2004

FCO 26/1215, Approach to Europe, 15th February 1972, Anthony Royle, later Lord Fanshaw, National Archive, Kew

FCO 30/1048, European Integration (effects on sovereignty), 1971, National Archive

Gaitskell Papers (Bilderberg) University College, London, Library

Gold Warriors, Sterling and Peggy Seagrave

Government White Paper, Treaty establishing a Constitution for Europe', issued in September 2004

Hidden Hand, Chapter.16., The CIA's Federalist Operation: ACUE and the European Movement, Richard Aldridge, Nottingham University - 2001. Quotes at the end of this Bibliography.

Human Rights Act to a Bill of Rights, Parliament web-site: www:parliament.uk

IBM and the Holocaust, Edwin Black, republished 2011

Lobster Journal, Robin Ramsay's, 1996 article in issue.cc, ISSN: 0964-0436

Lobster Magazine, Robin Ramsay

Magna Carta,

Mail on Sunday, 19th January 2003, Simon Walters (copy available this author)

Nazi Gold: The Merkers Mine Treasure by Greg Bradsher; Prologue Magazine, Spring 1999, Vol.31, No.1 US National Archives.

Neuordnung Europas German New World Order

OFFICIAL REPORT, Hansard: 26th June, 1950; Vol. 476. c. 2043

OSS, CIA and European Unity and Statecraft, Richard Aldridge, Nottingham University, Vol.8, No.1, March 1997

Paper 2004: '65% of Britain's laws made in Brussels', Nirj Deva, Conservative (House of Commons Library)

Representation of the People Act, 1832

Rights of Man, 1792 publication, Part III, Chapter III, page 32.

Separate Ways, Peter Shore, published in 2000

Shoe-horned into the EU, produced by this author, 2004

Spycatcher, Peter Wright

The Leviathan, Thomas Hobbes

The Act of Settlement

The Age', Tuesday, 31st March 1981

The British Constitution in the 20th Century by Vernon Bogdanor (British Academy Centenary Monograph)

The Conservative Europeanist, N.J. Crowson

The Constitution of the United Kingdom by Peter Leyland (Hart Publishing)

The English Constitution, Bagehot, Walter Bagehot, Parliament Bookshop, London

The EU and the Death of Local Government, Lindsay Jenkins

The European Movement, 1945-1953, Thesis, F.X. Rebattet – Bodleian Library, Oxford.

The Grand Remonstrance 1641

The Last Days of Britain, Lindsay Jenkins

The Wedge: The Secret war between the FBI and CIA, Mark Riebling, Simon and Scuster, June 2010

Time Out Magazine, Spring 1975

Tom Paine: A political life, John Keane, Bloomsbury.

Understanding a written part of our Constitution, The Coronation Oath, The Declaration and Bill of Rights 1688(9), John Bingley.

Union Now, Clarence Streit

Unlawful Governance, John Bingley

QUOTES from: 'The Hidden Hand' by Professor Richard Aldridge – first published in 2001 by John Murray.

Some extracts:

'The most remarkable US covert operation was vast secret funding of the European Movement'.

'In 1948, its [European Movement] main handicap was scarcity of funds; indeed it was bankrupt and close to collapse. The discreet injection of $4 million by the CIA between 1949 and 1960 was central to efforts ....'

'This covert contribution never formed less than half the European Movement's budget and, after 1952 it was probably two thirds'.

'The conduit for American assistance was the American Committee on United Europe (ACUE)

'The CIA funding operation through ACUE tells us a lot about the nature of American intervention in Western Europe'.

'.......Strikingly, the same small band of senior officials, many of them from the Western intelligence community, were central in supporting the three most important 'insider' groups emerging in the 1950s: the European Movement, the Bilderberg group and Jean Monnet's Action Committee for a United States of Europe'.

'The origins of CIA covert funding for European federalists may be traced back to the little-known figure of Count Coudenhove-Kalergi'.

The late Aaron Russo

Although American film producer, Aaoron Russo has not been quoted in this book, for an inside view of corporatist mentality, the reader can do no worse than watch the video he made shortly before his death:

http://www.dailymotion.com/video/x3qiv7_aaron-russo-sur-le-11-septembre-le_news

Index

1

1970 General election   4, 8, 61, 67,68,118
1975 referendum   95, 96, 97, 103, 104, 108, 129

2

24 Hours   10

3

30 Year Rule   81
38 Degrees   84

8

85 Frampton Street   121, 122, 124, 125

A

Abs, Hermann Joseph   144, 145
ACUE (American Committee for Un'd Europe)   v, vi, vii, 28
     83-85, 89, 90, 143
Adams, Mr   3, 5, 14, 17, 23, 24
Aldridge, Richard   v, 28, 101, 102
A letter to the Times   8, 17
Alexander, Michael   27
Allen, Lord of Abbeydale   107
Amsterdam Treaty   98
Anatoliy, Golitsyn   147
Anti-Federalist League   97
'anti-parliamentary'   64, 96
Approach to Europe   6, 9, 17, 56, 63
Ariane   44

Arnhem Bridge 142
Article 50 104
Atlantic Union (AU) 83, 84
Attlee, Clement 145
Aubiniere, General 40, 42, 43
Auschwitz 144

B

Bagehot, Walter xvi, xvii, xviii, 99, 135
Baldry, Tony 120
Ball, George 140
Bank of England 94
Barber, Anthony 4
Barclays Bank 55
BBC 5, 14, 17, 18
BBC Television Centre 121, 122
Beddington-Behrems, Edward 137, 138
Benn, Tony xviii, xix, 6, 63, 64, 96, 117, 148
Berle, Adolph v
Bernhard Prince iv, 137-139
Bilderberg iv, 28, 90, 121, 135-155
Bill of Rights 1688(9) xviii, 62, 100
Black Arrow 30-45
Black Knight 30
Blair, Tony 121, 124
Blue Streak 30, 38, 44
Blum, Leon v
Body, Richard 101, 106, 117
Bonn Embassy 22
Booker Column 44
Boothby, Lord 137
Boothroyd, Betty xviii
Borman, Martin 144
Branson, Richard 33
Breakfast Club 9, 10
Bridges, Tom 27

Britain in Europe (B in E)   109, 122, 123, 124
British America Tobacco (BAT)   126
British Council   16
British Embassy in Rome   22
British Leyland   52
Brown, Gordon   124-125
Bruges Group   97
Brussels' junkets   51
Brussels' office in London   6
Burke, Edmund   117
Burriss, Moffatt   142

C

Cabinet office file   40, 103, 108
Cameron David   xv, xvii, xviii, xx, 98, 104, 116
Cameron Bill of Rights   62
Campaign for an Independent Britain (CIB)   97
Carter, Harold   92
'cast iron guarantee'   98
Chancellor of the Duchy of Lancaster (Geoffrey Rippon)   1, 40
59, 61, 69, 72, 75, 106
Charlemagne Prize   41
Chase Manhattan Bank   94
Chatham House   54
Churchill, Winston   iv, v, vii, viii
CIA   v-vii, 8, 12, 28, 46, 47, 83, 89, 95, 98, 101, 105, 139, 147
Clarke, Kenneth   122, 124-126
Clinton, Bill   135
Cold War   xii, xiii, xiv, 84
Colombo, Emilo   31
Common Agricultural Policy (CAP)   ix, 25-31, 33, 38, 95, 98
Common Market (EEC)   4, 5, 10, 11, 50, 137-138, 148
Competition Commission'   164
Conduct of Referendum Bill   105
Confederation of British Industry (CBI)   6
Connaught Hotel   9

Conservative Group for Europe (CGE) — 5, 8, 12, 47
Conservative Party — xv, xix, xx, 61
Conservative Party Central Office (CCO) — 9, 22, 23
Conservative Research Department — 54
Consolidation (after joining EEC) — 95, 96
Constitutional Forum (which lead to Lisbon Treaty) — 125
Corfield, Frederick — 43
Coronation Oath — xvi, xvii
Corporates' Trade Union — 130
Council of Europe — vii, 138
Council on Foreign Relations (CFR) — v, 54
Crosby, J M — 59
Cuban blockade crisis — xiii
Cultural Relations Department (CRD) — 16

D

Davies, Denzil — 78
Davis, Evan — 121, 123
Davos (World Economic Forum) — xix, 130-134
Davies, John — 33
d'Estaing, Giscard — 125, 144
de Garperi, Aleide — v, 140
de Gaulle, General — viii, 4
de Gaulle's veto — 4, 46
de Manio, Jack — 18
de Villemarest, Pierre and Daniel — 138
Declaration and Bill of Rights (1689) — xviii
Declaration of Rights — 100
Dehomag — 91, 92
Democracy Movement — 97
Deutsche Bank — 144
Deutsches Museum — 38
Deva, Nirj — 81
Diamant — 38, 42
Divine Right of Kings — xvii, xviii
Dodds-Parker — 74

Donovan, General Bill   vi, xiii, 28, 84, 89
Douglas Home, Alec   27
Dual dating   100
Dulles, Allen   xiii, 89, 139
DuPont   93

E

ECA(72)   2, 14, 25, 29, 58, 68, 74, 95, 96, 97, 99, 103, 128
ECIU   3, 14, 15
Eden, Anthony   viii
EEC Information Unit   51, 56, 57
EID (European Information Department)   3, 13, 20, 49
Electoral Commission   100
euro   121, 122
European Coal and Steel Community (ECSC)   iv, vii, 25, 26, 46
European Communities Bill 1972   63, 65, 68, 72, 78
European Communities Information Unit (ECIU)   3, 14, 70
European Defence Community (EDC)   26, 28
European Integration Department   59
European League for Economic Cooperation (ELEC) 138, 139,144
European Movement (BCEM)   v, vi, viii, xiv xix, xxi, 8, 9, 12, 14
21, 25, 28, 46-55, 56-59, 61, 63, 83, 98, 121, 123, 143, 145
European Recovery Program   84
European single currency   121
European Union Constitution   62, 98
European Youth Campaign   46
Europeanness   36
EWCSW   16

F

Fanshaw, Lord   7
FCO 10/1048   62, 97
FCO 26/1215   6, 9, 17, 61
FCO 30/1048   2, 109-115
FCO 30/1061   71

Federal Reserve Bank of New York   94
Federal Union   83
First National Bank of New York   86, 93
First Reform Act (1832)   xv, xvii
'folkloristic' events   60
Foreign Princes, Persons, Prelates, States, or Potentates   99
Fortnightly Review   99
Frankfurt Consul General   22
Franklin, Benjamin   xiv
Franklin, George   v
Fraser, Hugh   81
French Mayors   58
Frere-Smith, Christopher   6, 19, 20
Friswell, Jack   117
Frost, Col.   142
'full hearted consent'   68, 80
Funk, Walter   iv
Fyjis-Walker, R.A.   21

G

Gaitskell, Hugh   107, 140, 142
Gardner, Dr Peter   xx, 97
General Belgrano   78
Gehlen, General Reinhard   xii, xiii, xiv
German Census Bureau   92
Globalisation   xv
Goldsmith, Jimmy   121
Goodson, Mr   40
Great Reform Act (see First Reform Act 1832)
Gregorian calendar   100
Gubbins, Major General   143
Guidance and Information Policy   15
Gummer, Selwyn   76

H

Hattersley, Roy	9, 10
Hancock, P. F.	22
Hartmarx Corporation	91
Healey, Denis	136, 138
Heath, Edward	viii, xx, 4-7, 8, 16, 18, 21, 23, 44, 68, 79
	80, 116, 119, 128, 157
Hibbert, Major Tony	142
Hobbes, Thomas	xvii
Hollerith (machine)	91, 92
Hordern, Peter	75
Hotel Bilderberg	142
Hotel Tafelberg	142
Howell, Lord Denis	13
Hurd, Lord Douglas	10, 35, 37, 70, 123, 160
Hurford-Jones, David	123

I

IBM	86, 91-93
IG-Farben	139
Indonesian President Sukarno	8
Information Administration Dept (IAD)	15, 21
Investor State Dispute Settlement	163
IRD (Information Research Dept)	5, 8, 11, 17, 18, 47, 51, 53
	54, 56
ITN	10
ITV	5

J

James II	xviii
Jay, Douglas	6, 63, 76, 77, 82, 96
Jellicoe, Earl	38
Jenkins, Roy	10, 96, 107
Johnson, Lyndon	28
Joint 'Statement of Purpose'	83

Jones, Hugh   14, 23
Joseph E. Seagram & Sons   86, 93
Jumelage (French Town Twinning)   58

K

'Keep Britain Out' (Campaign)   6, 19
Kissinger, Henry   138

L

Labour Committee for Europe   10, 23
Labour party   13
Labour Party   10, 16
Ladell, Dr.   144
Letter to the Times   8-10, 17
LIFE Magazine (October, 23rd 1939)   SEE BACK COVER
Lisbon Treaty   62, 98, 104, 125
Lloyds Bank   55
Lockheed Scandal   138
London's Earls Court   102, 107
Lord Marshall   123
Lord Pearson of Rannoch   128
Lord Portal of Hungerford   140, 142
Lord President of the Council (Whitelaw, William)   4, 5, 16, 17
Lupus erythematosus   147
Luxembourg 'Court'   128
Luxemburg Treaty   25

M

Maastricht Treaty   97, 98, 129, 160
MacFarquhar, Roderick   106
Magna Carta   62
Major, John   97, 129, 160
Mandleson, Peter   xix
Marshal Aid   xx, 90, 145

Marshall, General George	84
Marshall Plan	xx, 84
Marten, Marten	14, 70, 78, 116-120
Maudling, Reginald	140
McCloy, John	28, 90
McGhee, George Crews	viii, 137
Macmillan, Harold	viii, xi, 4, 146, 165
Macmillan, Maurice	33
McShane Dennis	123
Meacher, Michael	135
Mendelson, John	76
Merck & Co	90
Messina Conference	viii
Meyer, Anthony	123
MI5	8
MI6	8
Ministerial Committee on Science and Technology	35-36
Millo, Colonel R.W.	32
Monarchical government	166
Monnet, Jean	vii, 5, 25-29, 138
Monopolies and Mergers Commission	164
Morland, Mr	3
Morris, Alfred	80
Mouvement Européen	58

N

National Counting Officer	107
NEERA	66
Neuordnung Europas	iv
New World Order	xv
New York Times	135
News at 10	10
Nice Treaty	98
Noakes David	2, 76, 109, 110
Nobbling	11
non-binding referendum	104

non-binding, retrospective referendum	95
North Atlantic Free Trade Area (NAFTA)	84
North East England Regional Assembly	66

O

Oath of Office	99
Office of Strategic Studies (OSS)	v, xiii, 28
Onslow, Mr	43
Oram, Bert	74
Orwell, George	162

P

Paine, Thomas	xv, xvi, 166
Panorama	10
Parliament Act 1911	xvii, xxviii
Parliament bookshop	xix
Parliamentary Unit	24
Paxman, Jeremy	69
PEP	54
Pitt the Elder	xviii
Poll of polls	67, 95, 100
Porton Down	147
Powell, Enoch	6, 22, 23, 74, 79, 117
Prchal Eduard	144
President Kennedy	28
President of the Council	16
President Pompidou	6, 33, 36, 39, 42, 109
Presidential Medal of Freedom	28
Pressure in constituencies	70, 116-120
Prince Bernhard	iv, 134-139
Prior, James	79
Pro-EU Conservative Party	xx
Profile of a pro-European	156-159

Q

Qualified Majority Voting 75, 129
Queen in Parliament xviii, 62

R

Ramsay, Robin 107, 148
Rebattet, Francois Xavier vi, 83, 84, 85
Rebattet, George vi, 85
Reddaway, Norman 5, 8, 11, 12, 48, 59, 116
Referendum Act 104
Referendum propaganda 98
Reform Treaty 125
Regionalisation Programme 66
Remington Rand, Inc 86, 91
Representation of the People Act, 1832 x
Retinger, Dr. Joseph iv, v, vi, 137-139, 140-142, 149
Rhodes' scholar 83
Rights of Man xvi
RIIA 54
Robens Alfred 140
Robert, Owen J 83
Roberts, Alice (BBC Coast) 32
Rockefeller, David 88, 93, 135, 138, 135
Rockefeller, James Stillman 94
Rockefeller, John D. 93
Roosevelt, President Franklin. D (footnote) 83
Royal Aircraft Establishment 30
Royle, Anthony 6, 9-10, 17, 48, 51, 52, 56
Rusk, Dean 140
Rykens, Dr Paul 139

S

Salamandar Affair 144
Samuel Cabot Inc 90
Sandys, Duncan v, vi, vii, 25, 83

Schlitz Brewing Co   86, 91
Schuman Plan   vii
Scout Launcher   38
Shoe-horned into the EU   xix, xxi, 2, 8, 11, 81
Shore, Peter   viii, 6, 72, 73, 74
Sikorski, General Wladyslaw   iv, 138, 144
Simcock, Mr   20
Single European Act of 1986   75, 129
Sked, Alan   97
Slatcher, W. K.   20
Sovereignty and the European Communities   109
Soviet bloc   83
Soviet Union   xiv, 84
Spaak, Paul-Henri   iv, v, vii, 25
Spearing, Nigel   75, 76
Special Operations Executive (SOE)   8, 143
Spring Reception   121
Standard Oil   86, 93
Statement of Purpose   83-85
Steel, David   105, 106
Steering Committee (Bilderberg)   136, 140
Stevens, John   xx, 157
St John-Stevas, Norman   65, 70, 71, 118, 119
Stewart, Marshall   10, 11
Strategic Partners   130
Streit, Clarence   83
Suez   viii

T

Taylor, Ian   123
Taylor, John   119
Taylor, Teddy   69, 79, 116
Thatcher, Margaret   17
The Leviathan   xvii
The 'what if' conundrum   104

The Act of Settlement	xvi
The Act of Supremacy	99
The British Constitution	xvi
The Chase Manhattan Bank	94
The Economist	55
The English Constitution	xvi, 99, 135
The Federal Reserve Bank of St. Louis	94
The NFU	55
The Secrets of Bilderberg	138
The St. Louis Fed	94
The Times	52
The written Constitution	97
Thomas Paine test	xvii, 165
Time Magazine	135
Time Out magazine	101
Today	10, 11
Tory European Network (TEN)	123
Town Twinning	58-60
Treaty establishing a Constitution for Europe	1
Treaty of Accession	73, 75
Treaty of Lisbon (see Lisbon Treat)	
Treaty of Luxembourg	69, 72, 73
Treaty of Paris	46
Treaty of Rome	viii, 137
Trethowen, Ian	10, 18
Trojan Horse (Town Twinning)	58
Truman, President Harry	xiii
TTIP (Trans Atlantic Investment Partnership)	84, 121, 163
Tucker, Geoffrey	xx, 4, 9, 10, 18, 46
Turin Consul	22

U

UK Independence Party (UKIP)	97, 104, 164
un-British	64, 96
Unlawful Governance	xvii
USSR	xiv

V

Van Zealand, Paul   iv, 139
Vietnam War   84
Virgin Galactic   33

W

Waffen SS   xiii
Walters, Simon   16
Warren Commission   28
Washington Post   135
Watson, Thomas   86, 91, 92
Wedgewood Benn   64
Wellington Duke of   xv
Westminster Bank   55
Whitehall corridors of power   29
Who runs Britain?   79
Wilson, Harold   viii, 4, 32, 65, 72, 79, 80, 96, 129, 148
Wilson Government   98
Wistrich, Ernest   5, 9
Woman's Hour   10
Woodward, Shaun   70, 120
Woomera test range   30, 32
World at One   10
World Economic Forum (see Davos)
Wright, Peter   84, 147

Y

Young, Hugo   9

Z

Zyklon 'B'   93